YOU CAN TEACH YOURSELF® ELECTRIC BASS

By Mike Hiland

I0792717

Online Audio & Video

Audio
www.melbay.com/94358EB
Video
dv.melbay.com/94358
YouTube
www.melbay.com/94358V

Audio Contents

1 Introduction (:58)
2 Narration (:29)
3 Tune Up/Page 6 (1:09)
4 Finger Exercise/Page 11 (:49)
5 Exercise 1A-2B/Page 12 (2:33)
6 Narr. & Ex. 3-6/Page 13 (1:08)
7 Narr. & Ex. 7-10/Page 14 (1:16)
8 Narration/Page 15-18 (:22)
9 Clicks (:36)
10 Ex. 1-4/Page 20-21 (1:45)
11 Narr. & Ex. 1-5/Page 22-24 (2:53)
12 Narr. & Ex. 1-4/Page 25-26 (2:21)
13 Exercise 5 & 6/Page 27 (:58)
14 Narr. & Ex. 1-4/Page 28-29 (2:17)
15 Exercise 5-8/Page 30-31 (2:31)
16 Narration/Page 32-33 (:18)
17 Narration/Page 34 (2:47)
18 Narration/Page 35 (1:57)
19 Narr. & Ex. 1-2/Page 37 (:55)
20 Narr. & Ex. 1-3/Page 38 (1:11)
21 Exercise 4-8/Page 39-40 (2:01)
22 Narr. & Scales/Page 41-42 (:16)
23 C Scale/Page 43 (1:26)
24 Narr. & Scale/Page 44-46 (1:00)
25 A Scale/Page 49 (:27)
26 Narration/Page 51-54 (:48)
27 A Scale/Page 55 (1:10)
28 A Pentatonic Scale/Pg. 58-61 (:49)
29 Scales/Page 62-64 (:26)
30 Scales/Page 65 (:51)
31 A Blues Scale/Page 67 (:37)
32 Page 68 (:27)
33 Page 69 (:45)
34 Narr. & Exer. 1-3/Page 70-82 (:50)
35 Exercise 4-8/Page 71-72 (:50)
36 Exercise 9-13/Page 73-74 (:57)
37 Exercise 14-17/Page 74-75 (:46)
38 Exercise 18-22/Page 76-77 (1:02)
39 Exercise 23-28/Page 78-79 (1:06)
40 Exercise 29-33/Page 79-80 (:58)
41 Exercise 34-39/Page 80-82 (:51)
42 Exercise 40/Page 82 (:59)
43 Narration/Page 83-85 (:13)
44 Slap 1/Page 86 (1:29)
45 Slap 2/Page 87 (1:53)
46 Slap 3/Page 88 (:51)
47 Slap 4/Page 89 (:36)
48 Slap 5 & 6/Page 90 (:37)
49 Slap 7/Page 91 (:26)
50 Narration (:17)
51 Slap 8-11/Page 92-93 (1:41)
52 Narr. & Slap 12-16/Pg. 93-94 (1:17)
53 Slap 17-18/Page 94-95 (:34)
54 Narr. & Slap 19-21/Pg. 95-96 (:50)
55 Narr. & Slap 22-24/Pg. 97-98 (:51)
56 Narr. & Slap 25-27/Pg. 98-99 (1:32)
57 Narr. & Slap/Pg. 100-101 (:28)
58 Exercise 1-2/Page 102 (:29)
59 Narr. & Ex. 3-4/Pg. 103-105 (1:13)
60 Exercise 5/Page 104 (:27)
61 Exercise 6/Page 105 (:58)
62 Exercise 7/Page 107 (:33)
63 Exercise 8/Page 107 (:32)
64 Exercise 9/Page 107 (:31)
65 Exercise 10/Page 108 (:30)
66 Exercise 11/Pg. 108-109 (:35)
67 Exercise 12/Page 110 (:16)
68 Exercise 13/Page 111 (:25)
69 Exercise 14/Page 111 (:26)
70 Narration/Page 112 (:11)
71 Exercise 14/Page 113 (:18)
72 Exercise 15/Page 113 (:14)
73 Exercise 16/Page 113 (:14)
74 Narr. & Ex. 17/Page 114 (:26)
75 Exercise 18/Page 115 (:13)
76 Exercise 19/Page 115 (:16)
77 Narration/Page 116-117 (:34)
78 Narration/Page 117 (:16)
79 Exercise 21/Page 118 (:20)
80 Narr. & Ex. 22/Page 119 (:20)
81 Exercise 23/Page 120 (:18)
82 Exercise 24/Page 120 (:21)
83 Conclusion (:38)

MEL BAY®

WWW.MELBAY.COM

Contents

HOW TO USE THIS BOOK **4**
THE PARTS OF THE ELECTRIC BASS **5**
TUNING THE BASS **6**
PLAYING TECHNIQUE **8**
Left-Hand Techniques 8
Right-Hand Techniques 9
FINGER EXERCISES **11**
THE BASICS OF READING MUSIC **15**
Reading Music 18
Electric Bass Fingerboard Chart 19
Notes on the E-String 20
Notes on the A-String 22
Notes on the D-String 25
Notes on the G-String 28
Sharps, Flats, and Naturals 32
Key Signatures 33
Eighth-Note Studies 34
Dotted Notes 35
Sixteenth-Note Studies 35
Triplets 37
A FEW POPULAR BASS LINES **38**
SCALES **41**
More Scale Stuff 57
BASS LINES AND FILLS **70**
Walking Bass Lines 78
SLAP-AND-POP TECHNIQUE **83**
Left-Hand Technique 85
Slap Exercises 85
Pop Exercises 88
Technique Exercises 91
Simple Rhythm Patterns 92
More Rhythm Patterns 93
Hammer-Ons and Pull-Offs 95
RIGHT-HAND HAMMERING TECHNIQUE **100**
Right-Hand Technique 100
Left-Hand Technique 101
Right-Hand Hammering 101
Scales and Scale Patterns 112
Using More Than One Right-Hand Finger 117

Foreword

Let me start off by saying "Congratulations!!" Congratulations on your choice of the electric bass. You've chosen an instrument that is not only crucial to contemporary music but is also experiencing the most exciting developmental period in its history!! Listen to the radio and your favorite records — the bass is no longer mixed way in the back! It's right out front, driving the entire sound. Now, that's exciting!

Also, the development of new playing techniques, like slap and pop and the right-hand hammering techniques, makes bass players just as noticeable in a band as the singer or lead guitarist. At last, some respect for the instrument that is the tonal support system for any piece of music!!

As it says in the title, this book allows you to "teach yourself" how to play the electric bass. I am a firm believer in learning the basics and building from the ground up. Therefore, we will start by learning how to read music. After that, to start playing something you will recognize, there will be some bass lines that I think you will find familiar. There will be a section on different types of scales, as they are the key to understanding which notes you can and should play to achieve different effects.

Then, we get nuts!! There are two detailed sections to teach you how to slap and pop and how to get started in the right-hand hammering technique which has become so popular today.

Through all of this, you must remember one thing: Have fun!!! Playing music can provide you with some of the greatest highs you may ever experience. So, have fun and enjoy!!

I'd like to thank Mr. William Bay for giving me the opportunity to share this information with you. Also, thanks to all my family and friends for their continued support and enthusiasm. A special thanks to George and Gloria Kaye and all at Kaye's Music Scene. A project like this doesn't happen without the support of those around you — and I couldn't have done it without you. Thanks!!

Well, what are you waiting for?? Shouldn't you be practicing right now??

Enjoy!
...... Mike

How to Use This Book

This book contains a lot of information. It is written for the bass player who only wants to learn how to play some familiar bass lines, as well as for the player who wants to learn details about music theory and how they relate to the bass guitar.

As mentioned in the foreword, the electric bass is in a very exciting developmental period. It used to be that the bass simply provided the "low-end" support for a song. Not any more, Jack!! Nowadays, there are songs that are based completely around the bass line! There are bass solos contained within songs. And there are bass players who are pushing the limits of bass playing with their incredible soloing skills (ever hear Jeff Berlin or Jaco Pastorius play?).

The key to that kind of playing is in both music theory and ear training. Ear training is something that is developed in an individual over a period of time. Music theory is something to be learned. This book offers you the opportunity to get a solid start on music theory.

On the other hand, the most important thing about learning to play the bass is to have fun! And there is nothing more fun than hearing yourself play bass lines that you have heard others play, as well as hearing yourself playing with other musicians.

So, if you're the player who wants to get right to it and start to play some bass lines, you can skip the sections on scales (pages 41–69) and continue on page 70. And then you can come back later and read up on scales! And if you want to go through the section on scales, you can do that, too, by going through the book in the order it is presented.

Do it however you want!! After all, it's your book! It's important to have fun and see yourself making progress. This book is designed to do both of those things, so take full advantage of it and have a great time!!

The Parts of the Electric Bass

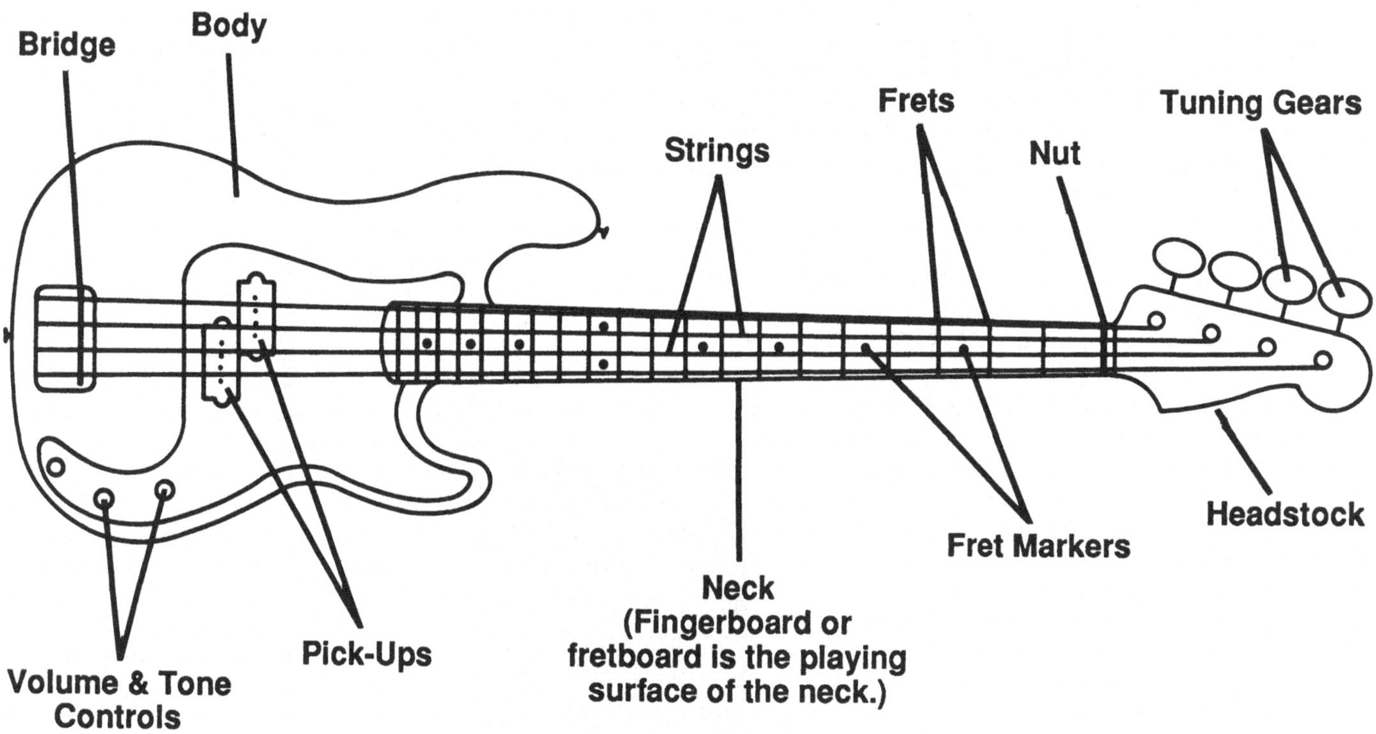

The four open strings of the bass will be the same pitch as the four notes shown in the illustration of the piano keyboard. Note that all of the strings are below middle C of the piano keyboard.

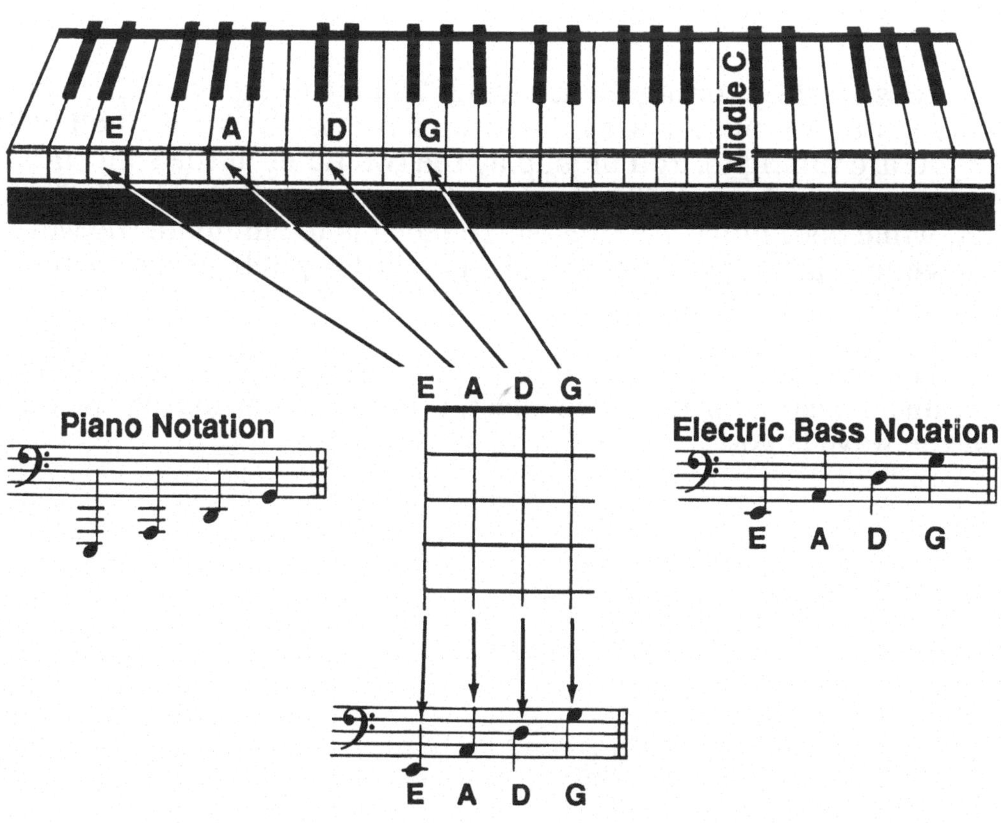

Tuning the Bass

Tuning the bass is done by first tuning one of the open strings to a pitch pipe, piano, or other musical instrument. First, you must know the names of the strings. The four strings on the bass are referred to by both numbers and letter names. They are as follows:

String Number	4	3	2	1
String Name	E	A	D	G

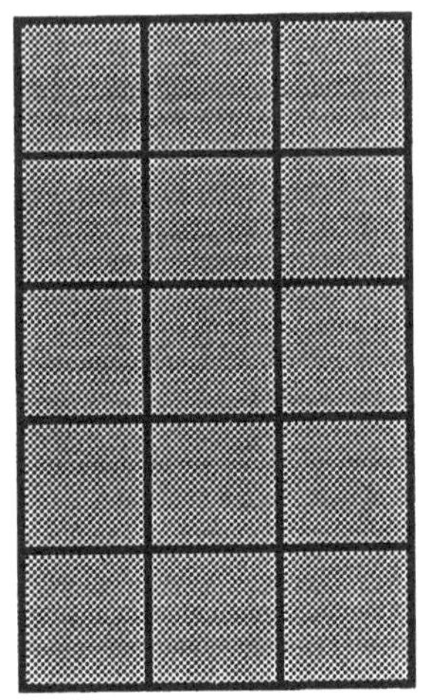

Let's start by tuning the E-string. When tuning the strings of the bass, you are listening to see if the bass string is the same pitch as the note you are tuning to. You must play the two notes at the same time. If they are not in tune, you will hear some dissonance, or what I call a "wave" effect, while both notes are ringing. The idea is to eliminate the wave. If the wave gets faster, the notes are farther apart in pitch. As it slows down, the notes are getting closer.

Try tuning the E-string to a piano, pitch pipe, or other musical instrument. Listen for the wave effect, and tighten or loosen the string until the wave is gone.

Once the E-string is in tune, tune the rest of the bass like this:

- **Play the open A-string. While it is ringing, play the note on the 5th fret of the E-string. Make sure that both notes are ringing at the same time. Tune the A-string either higher or lower until it is in tune with the note on the E-string. They should be the same pitch.**

- **Play the open D-string. While it is ringing, play the note on the 5th fret of the A-string. Make sure that both notes are ringing at the same time. Tune the D-string either higher or lower until it is in tune with the note on the A-string. They should be the same pitch.**

- **Play the open G-string. While it is ringing, play the note on the 5th fret of the D-string. Make sure that both notes are ringing at the same time. Tune the G-string either higher or lower until it is in tune with the note on the D-string. They should be the same pitch.**

The bass should now be in tune. Use this method any time the bass needs tuning.

Playing Technique

The goal of this section is to define proper hand placement and playing technique. You should apply these techniques at all time to ensure the development of good technique and avoid "bad habits."

Left-Hand Techniques . . . .

Smooth and efficient left-hand techniques are essential to good playing. It is very important to both the tone and feel of the music you are playing to be able to get to the necessary notes smoothly, accurately, and with the right touch. Here are the important things to remember about left-hand technique:

1. **The left-hand fingers should lie lightly across the strings and must always be relaxed. If your hand is stiff or tense, you will not be able to move your fingers easily, making it difficult to move smoothly, quickly, and accurately.**

2. **The left-hand fingers should be spread out slightly so that each finger covers one fret all the way across all four strings. Again, your whole hand should still be relaxed.**

3. **The left thumb should rest against the back of the neck, lining up with the space between the index and second fingers (L.H.). The thumb should be making contact with the neck just below the mid-point of the back of the neck. (If your neck has a stripe running the length of it, use that as a guide, with your thumb making contact with the bottom edge of the stripe.)**

NOTE: Never let your left thumb come up over the top of the neck. If you're grabbing the neck like a baseball bat, how are you going to move your hand quickly and smoothly up and down the neck?

So, with that in mind, here's how to place your left hand on the neck:

Lay your L.H. fingers across the strings so that each finger can cover one fret all the way across all four strings. (If your hands are smaller, it is okay to pivot your thumb so you can reach the E-string. Just make sure your fingers stay flat and relaxed.) Now, keeping your hand relaxed, bring your left thumb around to the back of the neck and position it between the first and second fingers, just below the mid-point of the radius of the neck. You're not squeezing or straining, are you??

Can your four L.H. fingers play four notes on the E-string in this position? Is it comfortable? You may have to get used to this feeling for a while because, if this is new to you, it may take a little while for your hand to get used to it. Practicing every day will help you get more comfortable with this technique.

Right-Hand Techniques . . . .

As you may have noticed, there are two ways to play the bass with the right hand — with the fingers or with a pick. Both have their advantages, so I would suggest learning both. First, let's talk about *playing with the fingers.*

1. **Anchor the right thumb either on a pick-up or on the low string on the bass. Anchoring the thumb in this way counter-balances the picking force of the right-hand (R.H.) fingers.**
2. **Picking is done with the first and second R.H. fingers. The important thing to remember is always to alternate the fingers in this order: 1–2–1–2–1–2–1–2.... It is very easy to get lazy and play simple parts with just the first finger, but BEWARE!! It's bad habits like this that will kill you in the long run. Believe me, I've been killed like this in a couple of areas, and it ain't no fun!**

3. **After a R.H. finger has picked a note, it should come back and touch the string below the string it just picked. (After playing a note on the A-string, the R.H. finger should touch the E-string.) When playing on the lowest string, let the finger come back and touch the right thumb (if it's not too far). Doing this with the R.H. fingers allows your fingers to subconsciously "know" where the strings are.**

Now, let's talk about playing with a pick. I'd recommend using the heaviest pick you can find because bass strings are very heavy, and thin picks will bend under the pressure of picking, resulting in a weak attack on each note that is picked. Here's the technique of *playing with a pick:*

1. **Hold the pick between the thumb and first finger so that it points in a direction that is 90 degrees from the direction of the fingers.**
2. **Pick the string using a "down stroke" across the string. Pick only one string at a time. To pick the next note, use an "up stroke" across the string. Always alternate down stroke, up stroke, down stroke, up stroke, etc....**
3. **You can use the heel of the right hand to "mute" the strings back by the bridge. This is a very common technique in rock bass playing. It helps keep unwanted notes from ringing.**

Finger Exercises

The following finger exercises will help develop the strength and dexterity you will need to set the world on fire! Practice them every time you pick up the bass. Also, experiment with some of your own exercises to help build strength in areas where you may find that your hands are weak.

Be sure to concentrate on the right- and left-hand techniques described earlier. It is very important that you do not fall into some bad habits. We all know how hard it is to break them!!

We will be using a number of different diagrams to help you understand where to play the notes. Here's an explanation of the diagrams used in this book:

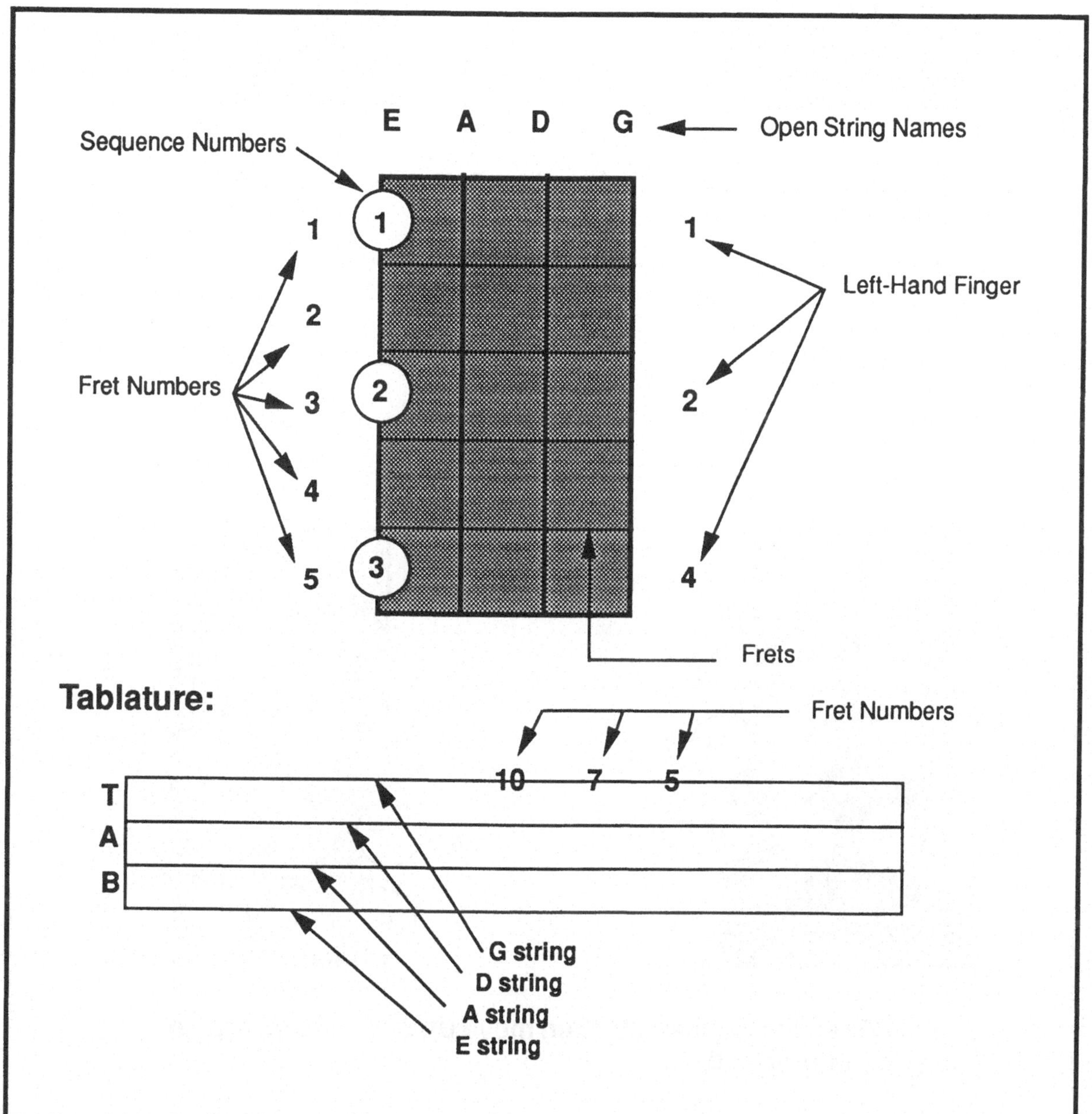

Finger Exercise #1a

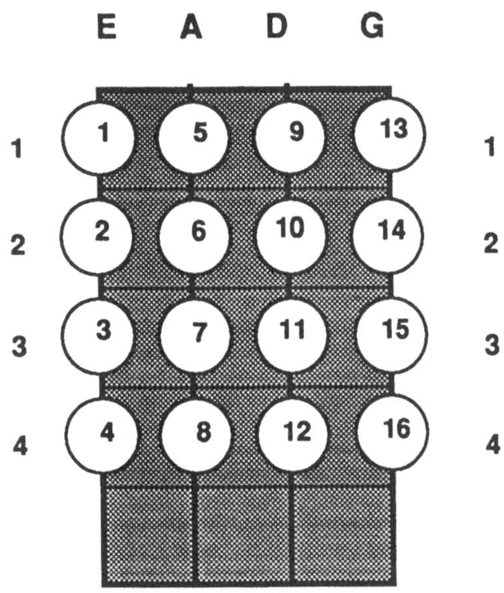

Finger Exercise #1b

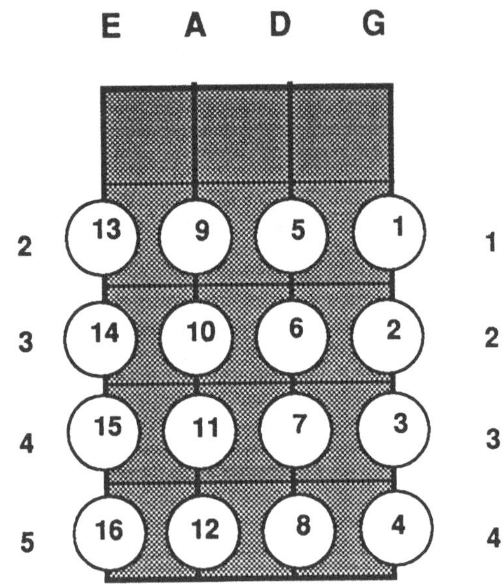

Play Exercise 1a, then 1b, then move up one fret and repeat until you run out of frets!!

Finger Exercise #2a

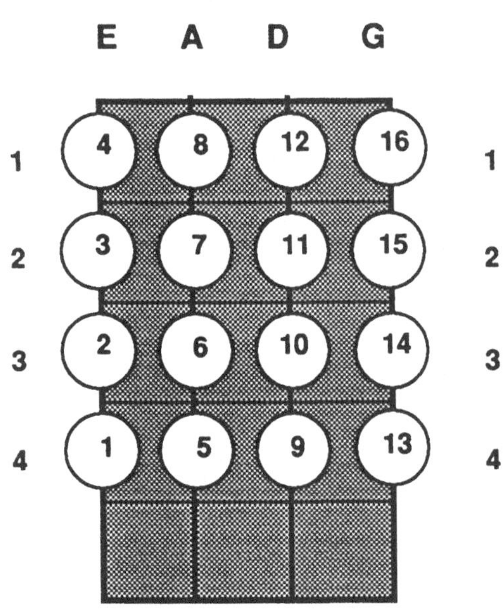

Finger Exercise #2b

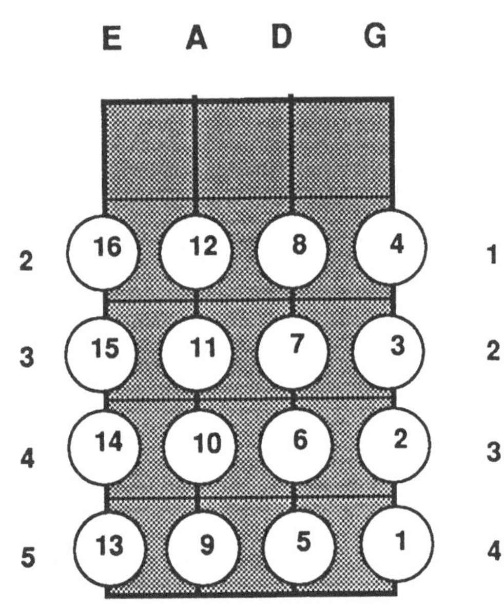

Play Exercise 2a, then 2b, then move up one fret and repeat until you run out of frets!!

Finger Exercise #3

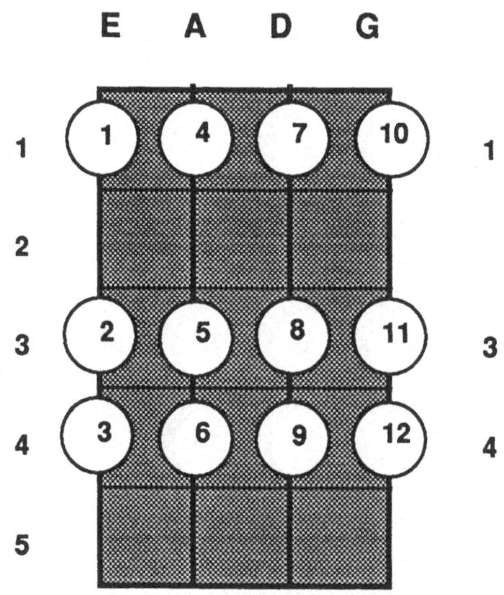

Finger Exercise #4

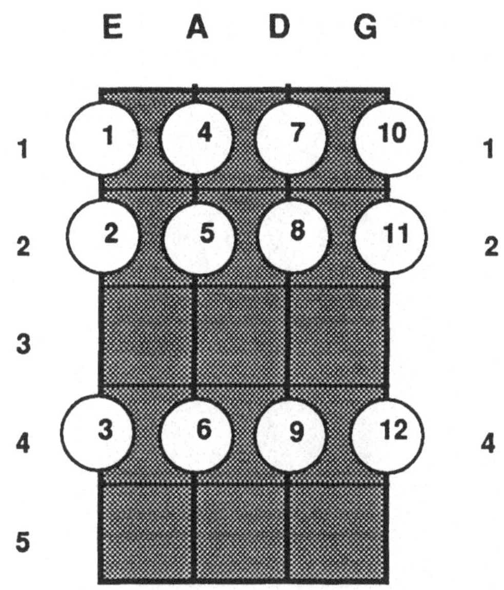

Play each exercise all the way up the neck as in Exercises 1 and 2.

Finger Exercise #5

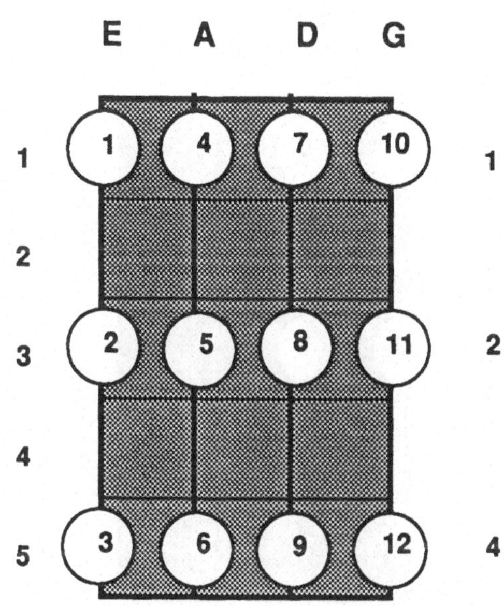

Finger Exercise #6

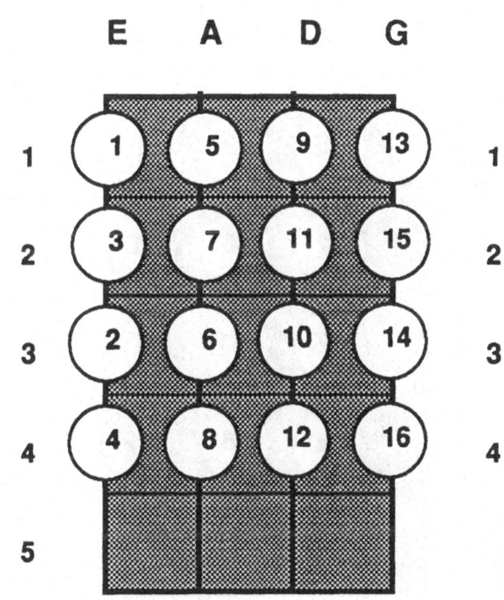

Play each exercise all the way up the neck as before.

Finger Exercise #7

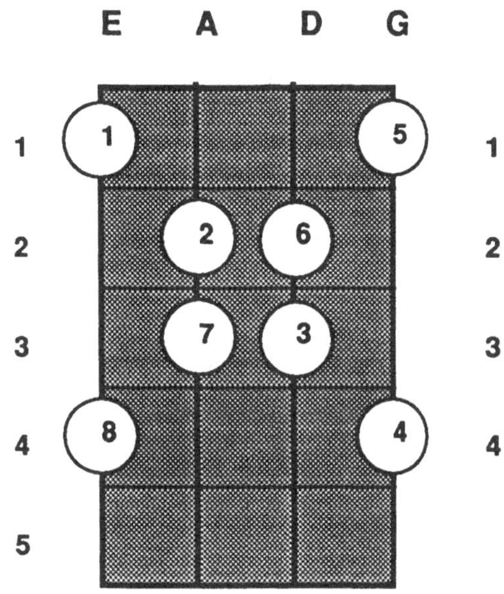

Finger Exercise #8

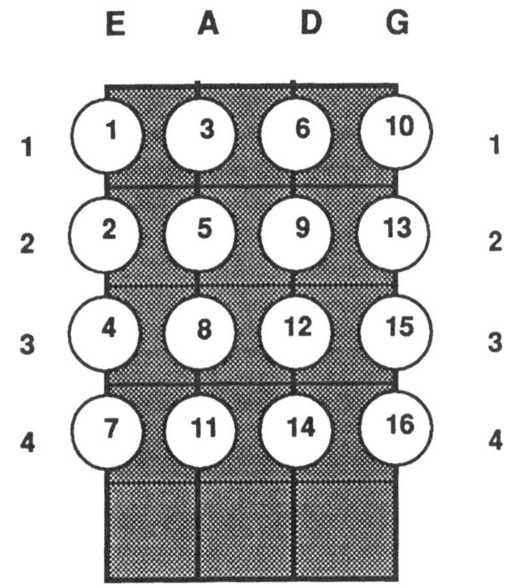

Play each exercise all the way up the neck as before.

Finger Exercise #9

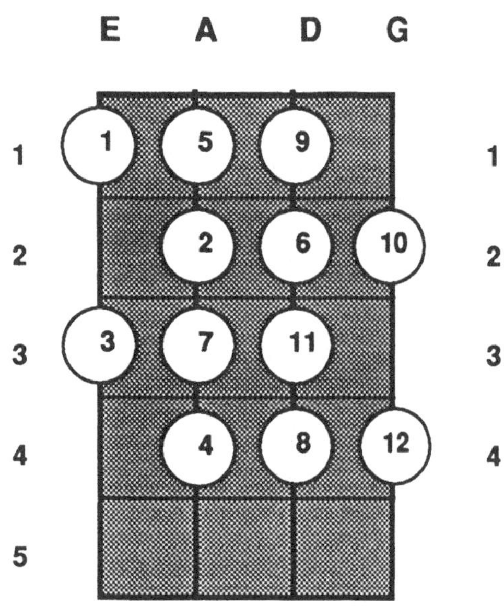

Finger Exercise #10

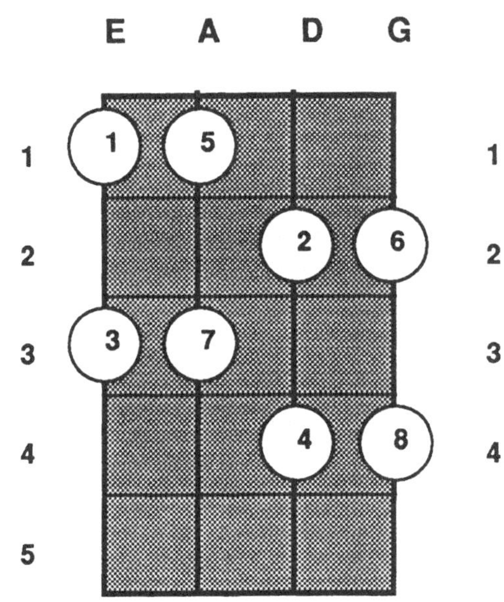

Play each exercise all the way up the neck as before.

The Basics of Reading Music

Written music tells you two things: 1) which note(s) to play and 2) how long to play the note(s). Other embellishments may be added, but that is basically what reading music is all about.

All music is written on a **STAFF** which is made up of five lines and the spaces that are created between the lines. Each line and each space has a letter name, or note name, associated with it. The letter names for the lines and spaces depend on whether the music is written in the **BASS CLEF** or the **TREBLE CLEF.** All bass guitar music is written in the bass clef. Examples of the bass clef and treble clef signs are shown below:

Treble Clef

Bass Clef

In the **BASS CLEF,** the lines are named G–B–D–F–A like this:

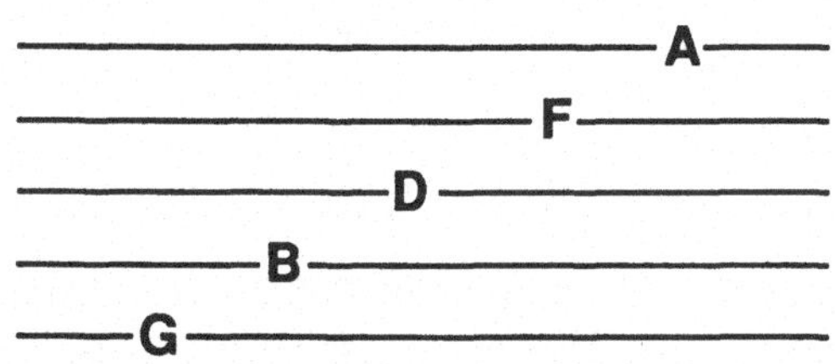

And the spaces are named like this:

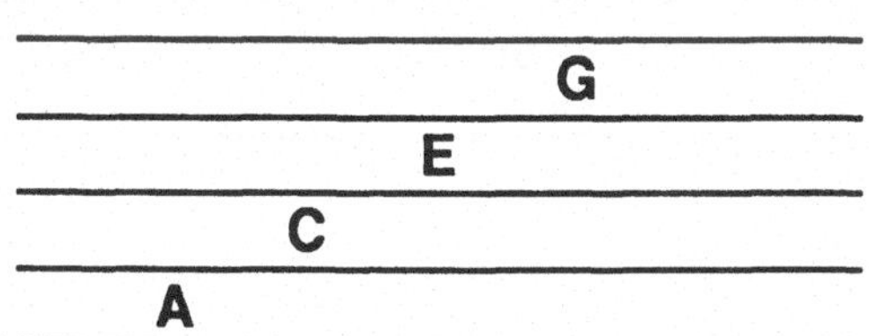

Notice that, when the names are placed on the same staff, the letter names are alphabetical, moving up the staff from bottom to top:

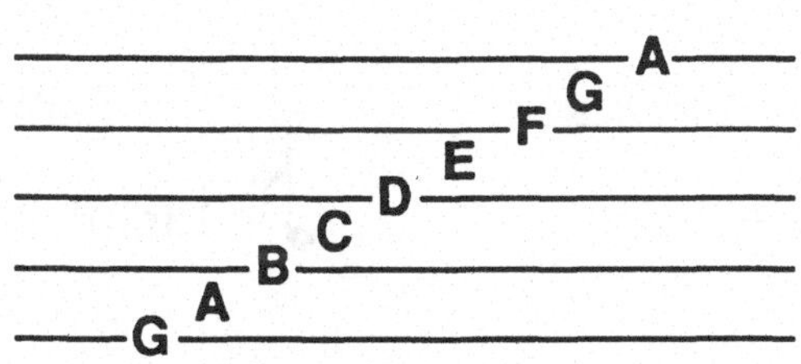

When a note is too high or too low to be placed on the staff, it is then indicated using lines and spaces that are created by extending the staff upwards or downwards. This is done by using **LEDGER LINES** as follows:

The staff is divided into **MEASURES** by vertical lines called **BAR LINES:**

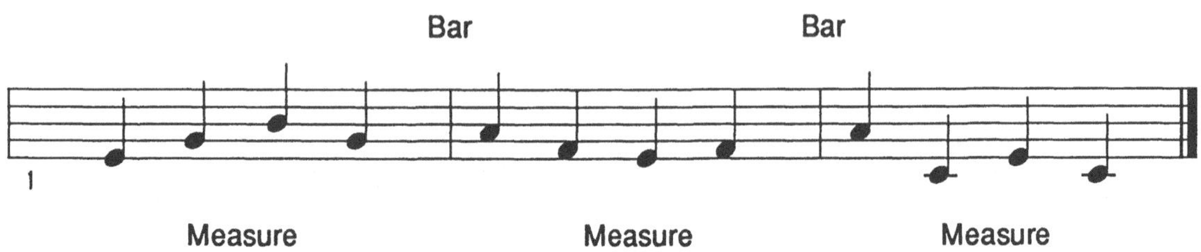

Music is a language. One way to help you understand how it is written is to compare it to the English language. In English, words are written in a sentence. In music, they are written on a STAFF. If there were no spaces between the words in a sentence, they would be very difficult to read. MEASURES and BAR LINES serve the same purpose as the spaces between the words in a sentence. They make it easier to read one small piece at a time. It's that simple!!

NOTES are the symbols that tell you which tone to play and how long to play it. Notes are placed on the staff, above the staff, and below the staff. The location of the note on the staff will indicate the pitch of the note. The actual shape of the note will indicate how long to play it. Here are what the different types of notes look like and what their values are:

𝅝 Whole Note = 4 beats　　𝅗𝅥 Half Note = 2 beats

♩ Quarter Note = 1 beat　　♪ Eighth Note = 1/2 beat

A REST is the opposite of a note; it is a period of time that you don't play. There are rests that are equal in length to their corresponding notes:

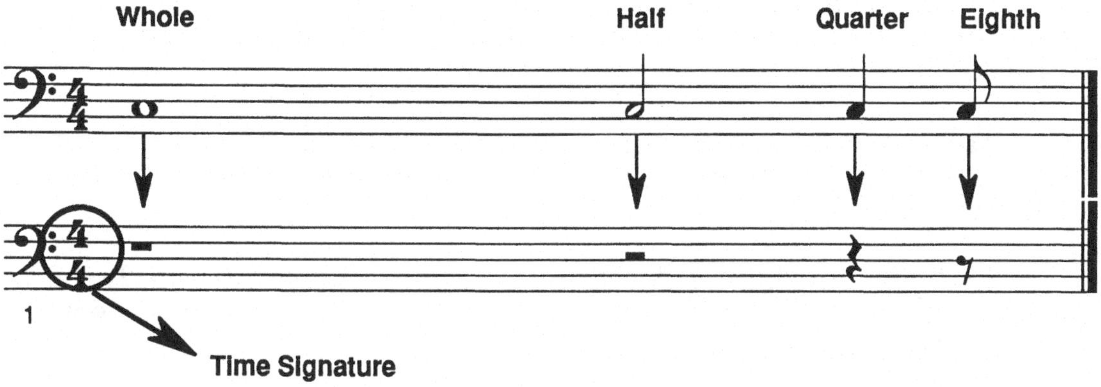

TIME SIGNATURES tell you how to count the beats in a measure. The top number indicates the *number of beats per measure.* The bottom number indicates the *type of note receiving one beat.*

The top number simply tells you how high you will be counting in each measure. If the top number is 4, you will count each measure as 1–2–3–4, 1–2–3–4, etc.... If it is a 3, you will count 1–2–3, 1–2–3, etc.... That's pretty simple, huh??

The bottom number's meaning can often seem confusing until you understand it. If the bottom number is 4, that means that a quarter note is counted as one beat. Because of the relationship between the different types of notes, that would mean that an eighth note would receive one half of a beat; a half note would receive two beats; and a whole note would receive four beats, exactly as explained before.

However, if the bottom number is 8, then all of the note values shift relative to the eighth note's new value of ONE beat. That is, the quarter note (which is twice as long as an eighth note) is now counted as TWO beats; the half note is counted as FOUR beats; and the whole note is counted as EIGHT beats. It's really just a different method of reading and writing music.

Reading Music

When you are first learning to read music, it is best to tap your foot and count the beats out loud as you play. Another way is to use a metronome, and count out loud with the clicks of the metronome.

The time signature tells you how you will be counting. In the example below, the time signature is 4/4, so you will be counting to 4 (1, 2, 3, 4, 1, 2, 3, 4, etc....) because the top number is 4.

In the first measure below, the whole note is played at exactly the same time as you count "1" (this is called "on one"), and the note rings as you count the rest of the measure (2, 3, 4 ...).

In the second measure, the first half note is played on "1" and, because it is two beats long, it rings through the second beat as you count "2." Then you play the second half note of the measure on "3," and it rings through the fourth beat as you count "4."

In the third measure, each note is played "on the beat"; or, each time you count a beat, you play a note at the same time and let the note ring until the next note is played (on the next beat).

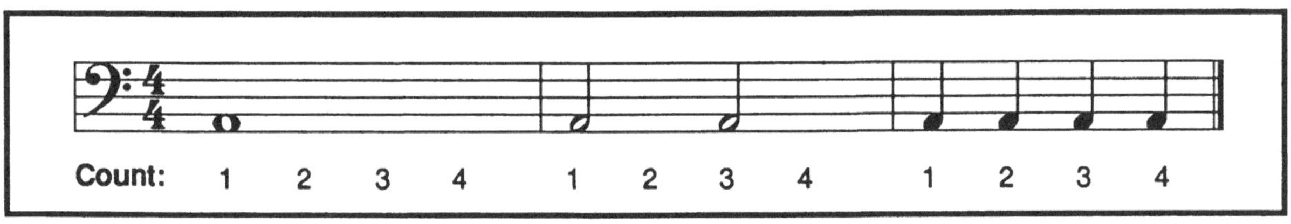

Okay, now that we're done with that...let's learn some notes!!

Electric Bass Fingerboard Chart

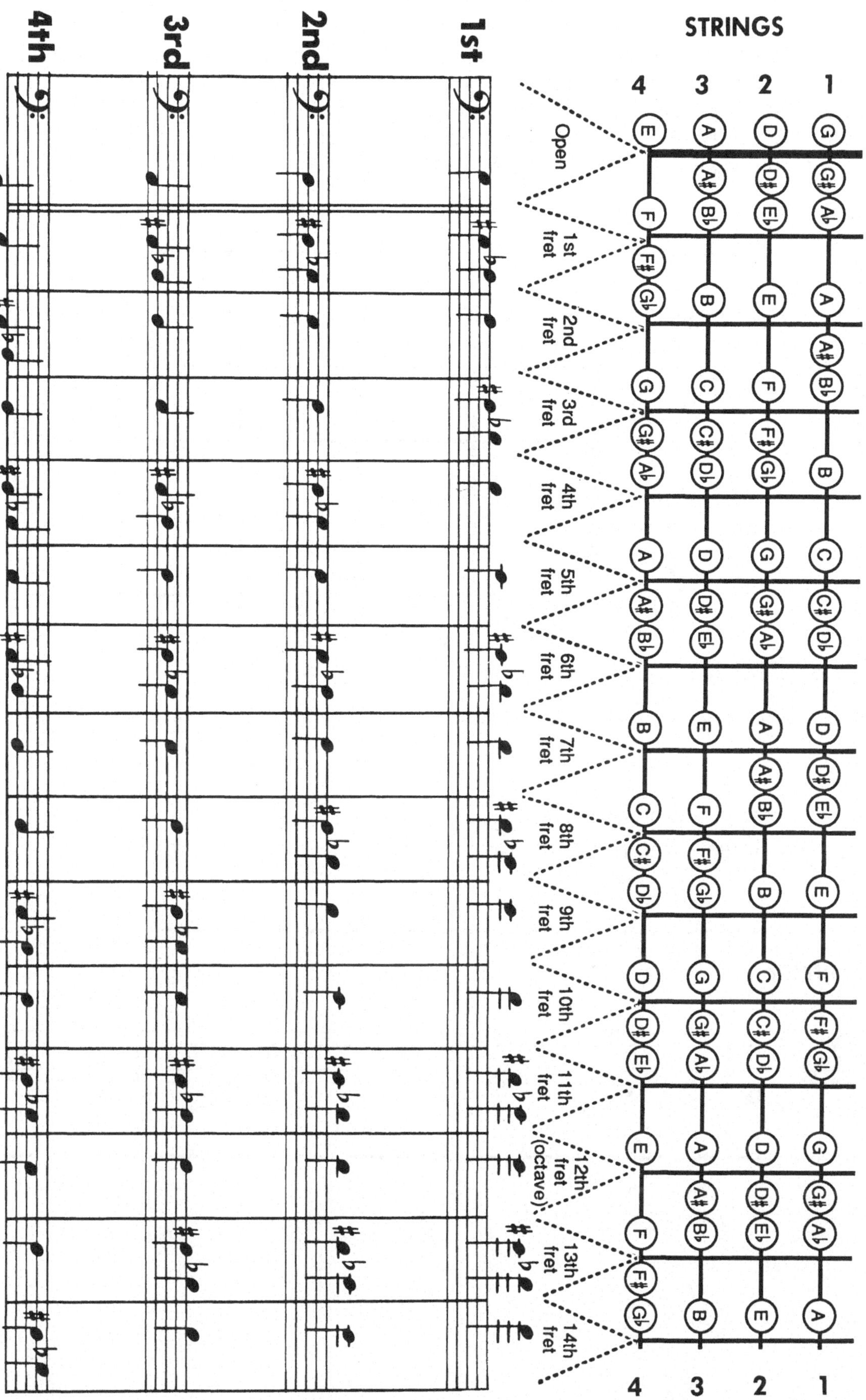

Notes on the E-String . . . .

First, we will learn three notes on the fourth or E-string. The notes are the open string, which is E; the first fret (F); and the third fret, which is G. Don't worry about the second fret right now. We'll cover that one later! Remember to follow the techniques described in the chapter on finger exercises when playing all of the following exercises.

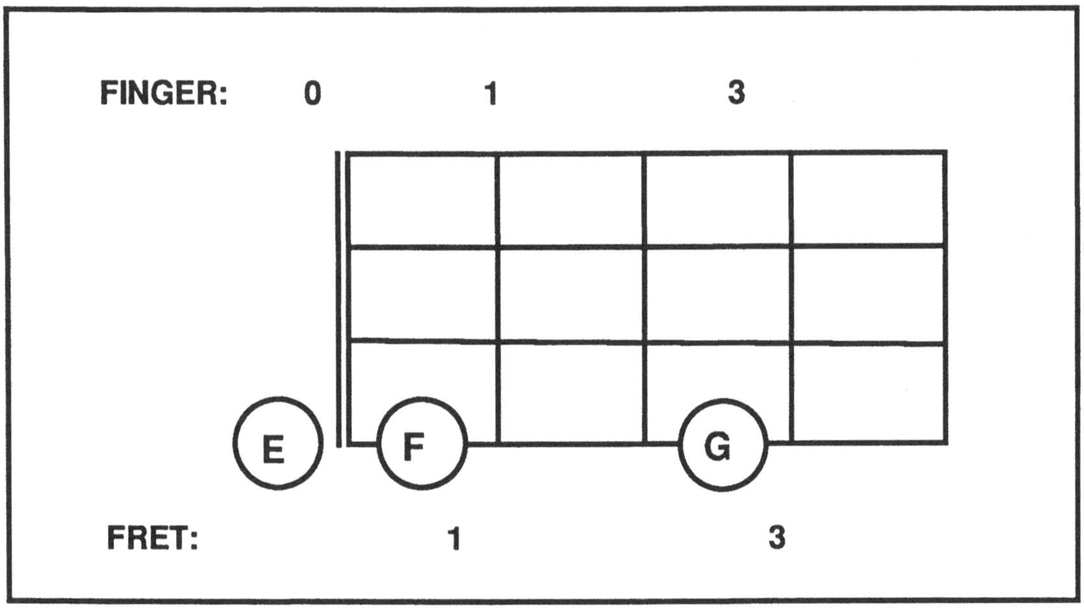

Play the following exercises slowly and carefully until you are able to play these three notes at "first glance" without hesitation.

Exercise 1

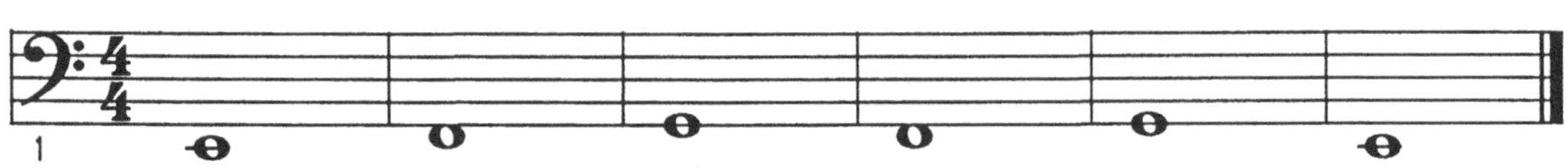

Exercise 2

Exercise 3

Exercise 4

Notes on the A-String . . . .

We will now learn three notes on the third or A-string. They are the open string, which is A; the second fret (B); and the third fret, which is C. Be sure to use the second finger for the B and the third finger for the C. Using the correct finger(s) is very important.

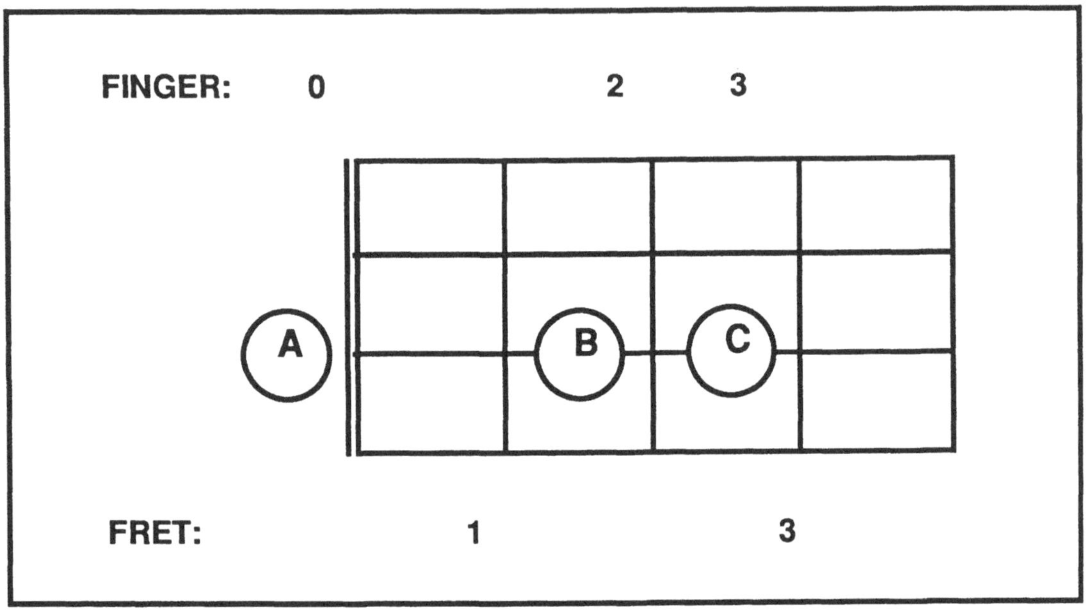

Play the following exercises until you can play the A, B, and C at first glance without hesitation. Concentrate on your right- and left-hand technique so you don't fall into any of those bad habits I was talking about!!

Exercise 1

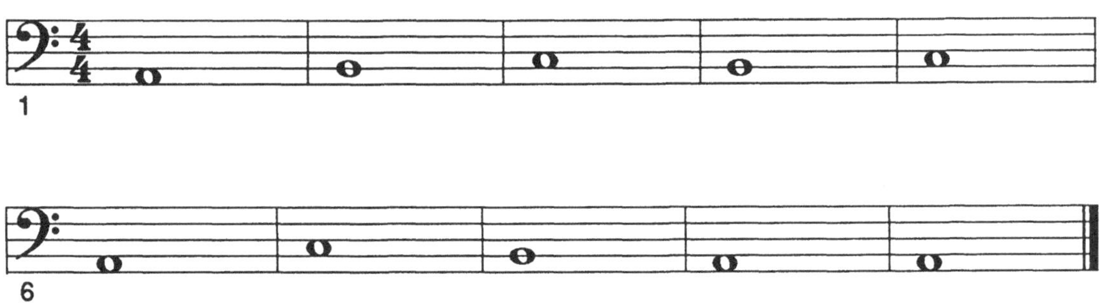

Exercise 2

Exercise 3

Exercise 4

Practice this exercise which uses the three notes on both the E-string and the A-string. Be sure that you can play this exercise all the way from beginning to end before continuing to the second-string exercises.

Exercise 5

Notes on the D-String

We will now learn three notes on the second or D-string. They are the open string, which is D; the second fret (E); and the third fret, which is F. Be sure to use the second finger for the E and the third finger for the F. Using the correct finger(s) is very important.

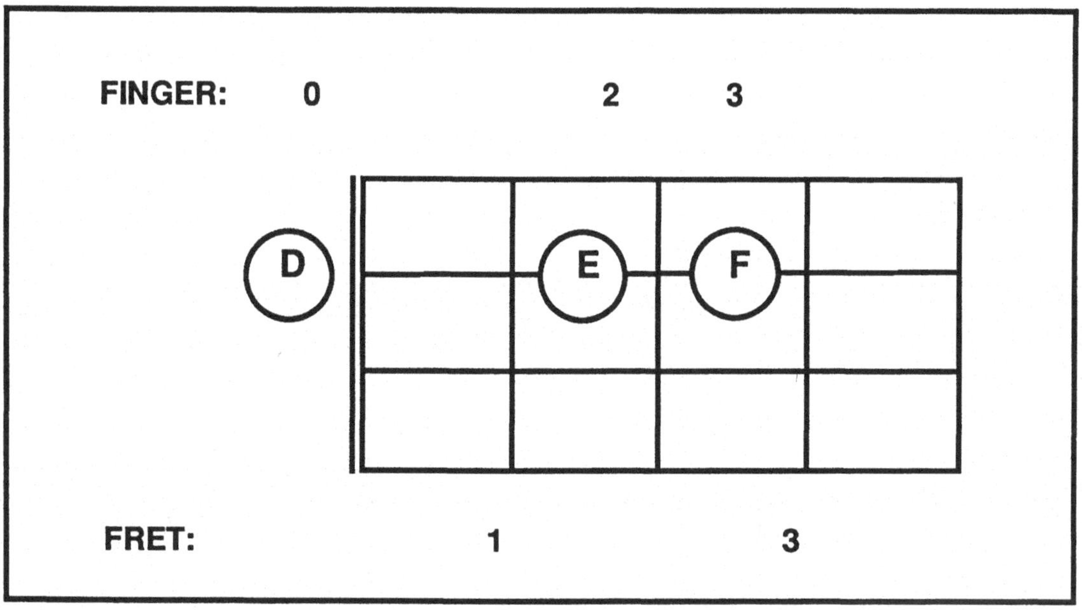

Play the following exercises until you can play the D, E, and F at first glance without hesitation. Concentrate on your right- and left-hand technique so you don't fall into any of those bad habits!

Exercise 1

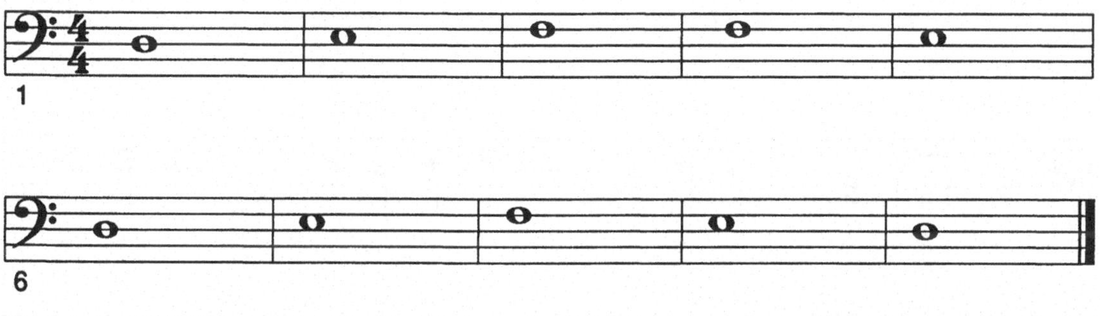

Exercise 2

Exercise 3

Exercise 4

Practice these exercises which use the notes on the E-string, A-string, and D-string. Be sure that you can play this exercise all the way from beginning to end before continuing to the first-string exercises.

Exercise 5

Exercise 6

Notes on the G-String

Now we will learn three notes on the first or G-string. They are the open string, which is G; the second fret (A); and the fourth fret, which is B. To play the A and B, you need to shift your left hand slightly so that your first finger can play the second fret, the second finger plays the third, etc.... In this position, the first finger will play the A and the third finger will play the B.

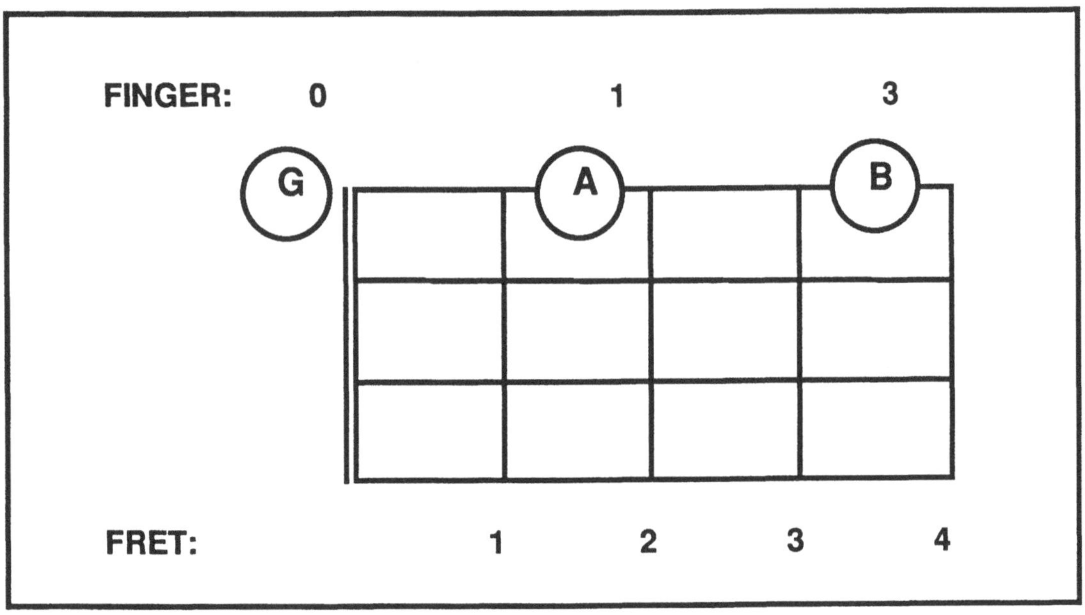

Play the following exercises until you can play the G, A, and B at first glance without hesitation. Concentrate on your right-hand technique, and make sure your left hand is in the correct position when playing the open G, A (second fret), and B (fourth fret).

Exercise 1

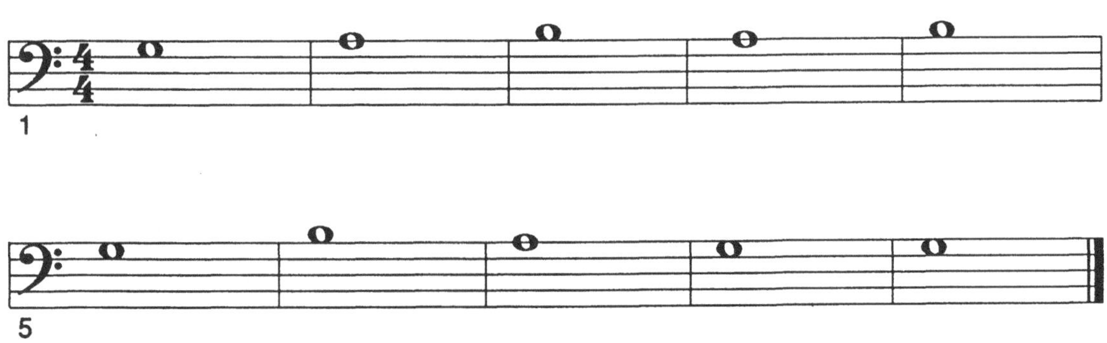

Exercise 2

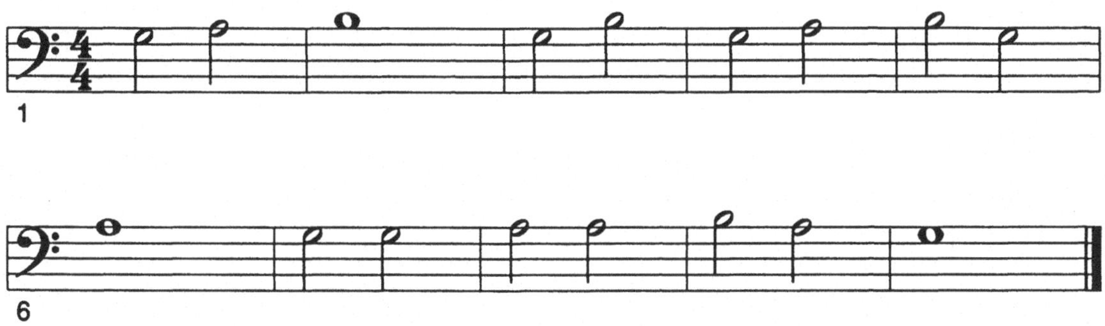

Exercise 3

Exercise 4

Practice the following exercises which use the three notes you have learned on each of the four strings. Watch your right- and left-hand technique carefully (tired of hearing that yet?). And, when changing from the E-, A-, or D-strings to the G-string, be sure you are changing position slightly to play the A and B on the G-string with the first and third fingers.

Exercise 5

Exercise 6

Exercise 7

Exercise 8

Sharps, Flats, and Naturals

Now let's talk about those notes that fall "in between" two other notes. You've already noticed that some notes are two frets apart, and some are only one fret apart. This distance is called the **INTERVAL.** Notes that are one fret apart are called **HALF STEPS,** while notes that are two frets apart are called **WHOLE STEPS.** (Two halves make a whole, even in music!!)

The notes that fall in between two notes which are a whole step apart have names that make them a little different from the A, B, C, D, E, F, and G that we have learned so far. A, B, C, D, E, F, and G are called **NATURAL** notes. To identify a note that is not a natural note (it falls *between* two natural notes), we use the descriptors **SHARP** and **FLAT.** Here are the definitions:

♯ = Sharp	⟶	Raises natural note by one half step
♭ = Flat	⟶	Lowers natural note by one half step
♮ = Natural	⟶	Cancels previous sharp or flat

The following diagram should help:

Key Signatures . . . .

Needless to say, it could get pretty confusing trying to read a whole bunch of sharps and flats in a piece of music. What if *all* of the notes were either sharp or flat?? Wouldn't it be nice if you could be told ahead of time that the F's are always sharp? Or that the B's are always flat? Well it's possible!! I would like to take credit for it, but a very long time ago someone else created the **KEY SIGNATURE.**

The key signature is located at the beginning of every staff of music immediately after the bass clef symbol. The following key signature is telling you that every F and every C should be played as F♯ and C♯.

While the key signature changes all occurrences of the affected note(s) throughout the piece of music, a natural sign may be used to change it back to a natural note. *However*, the natural sign will only be in effect to the end of the measure that it is in. At the beginning of the next measure, the key signature is back in effect. Watch some of the tablature in the rest of this book to see occurrences of this!

Eighth-Note Studies ....

As mentioned earlier, eighth notes are one half of a beat long. Let's take a look at how eighth notes are read, counted, and played.

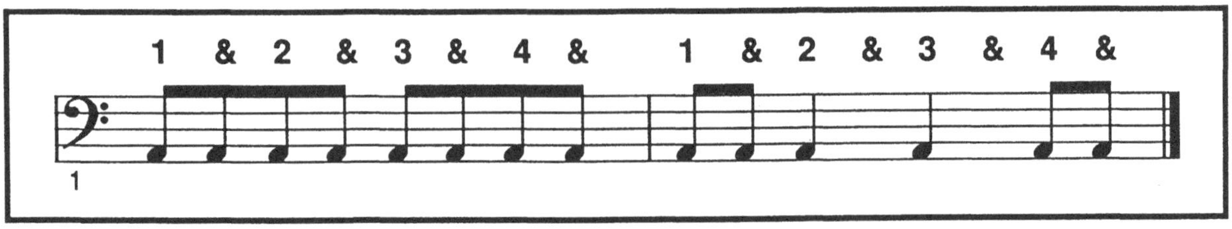

As you can see, eighth notes are played on the beat or exactly in between the beats. Let's try a study of a bunch of different eighth-note rhythm patterns:

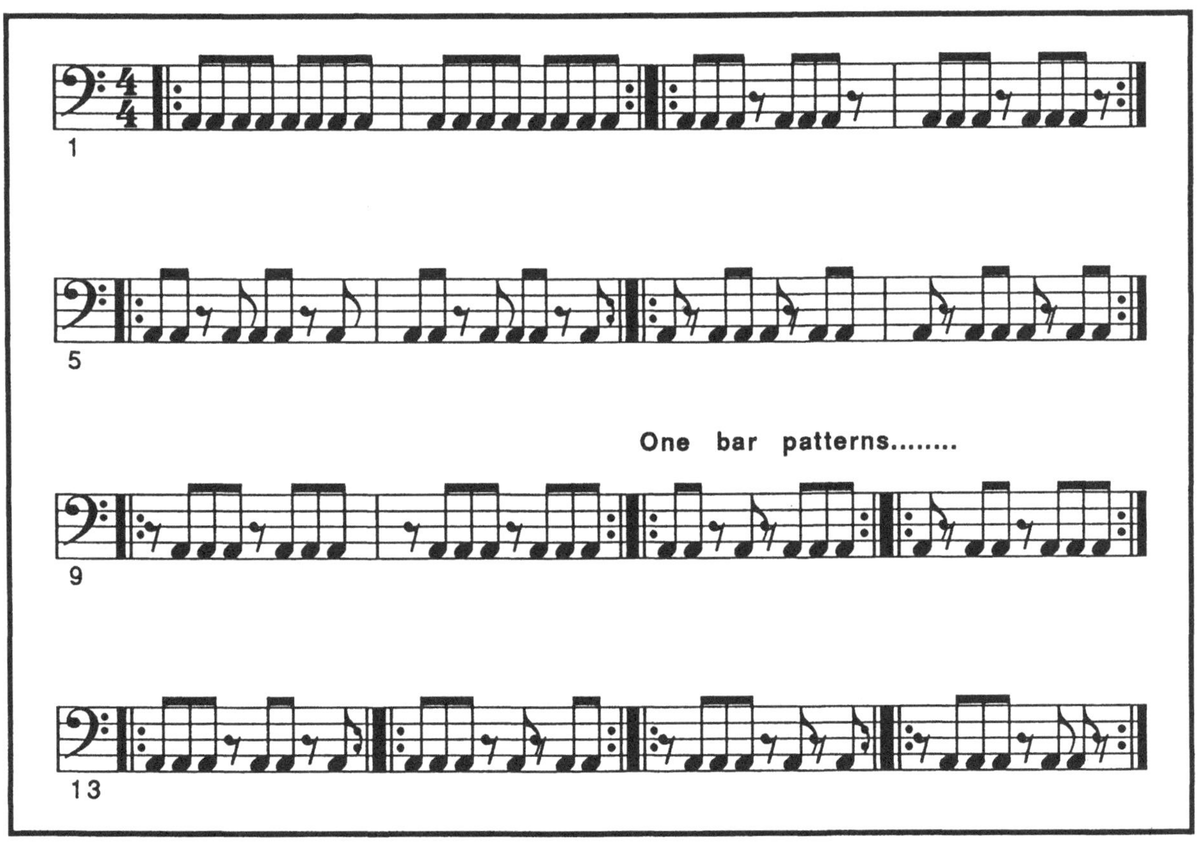

Dotted Notes ....

By placing a dot behind a note, the note's original value is increased by one half. That means that a quarter note, which is usually worth one beat, is worth one and one half beats when a dot is added to it. Here are some examples of how that works:

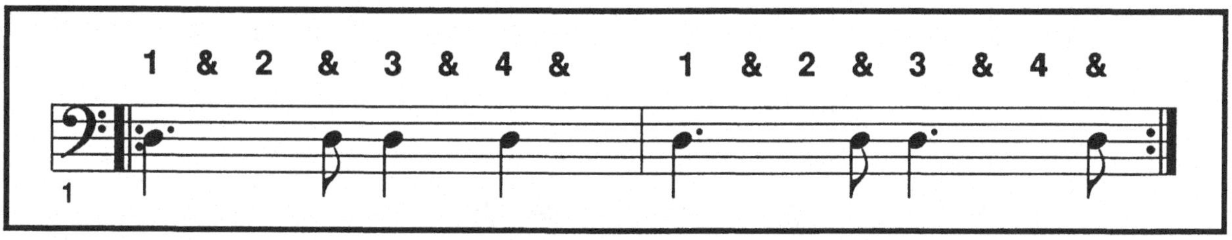

Sixteenth-Note Studies ....

Sixteenth notes are half as long as eighth notes. Thus, for every eighth note, there are two sixteenth notes. There are a number of different sixteenth-note rhythms to memorize. That way, whenever you see a particular rhythm pattern, you can remember what it sounds like and you won't have to try to read it — it's all memorized!! Let's take a look:

Play each of the following sixteenth-note rhythm patterns until you can play each note evenly and in proper time.

There is one final sixteenth-note rhythm pattern, as well. Practice it many times until you have it down. It is counted like this:

Triplets . . . .

There is one more rhythm pattern that we must talk about before I send you off to set your fretboard on fire. The idea behind **TRIPLETS** is for you to play three notes in the time period normally allotted for two. If they are eighth-note triplets, you would play three notes in the space of two eighth notes.

Here's a little help:

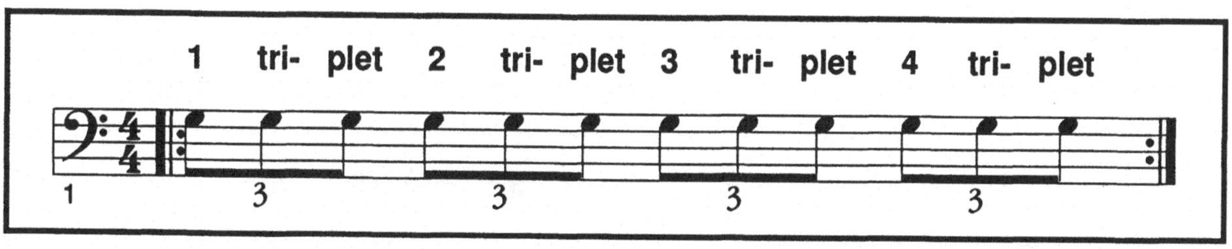

Try this over and over to get the hang of it....

A Few Popular Bass Lines

Here are a few popular bass lines that you may recognize. They are all a little different rhythmically, and they cover most of the neck. Have fun learning to play them!!

Exercise 1

Exercise 2

Exercise 3

Exercise 4

Exercise 5

Exercise 6

Exercise 7

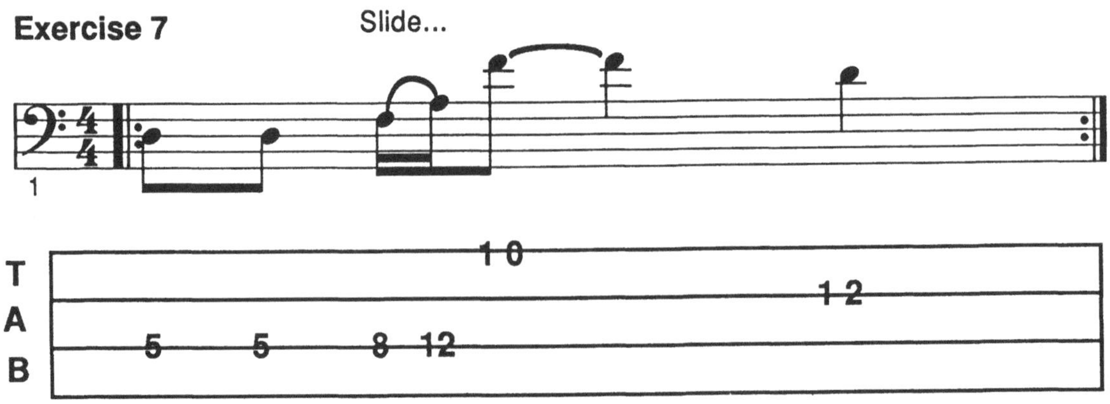

Exercise 8

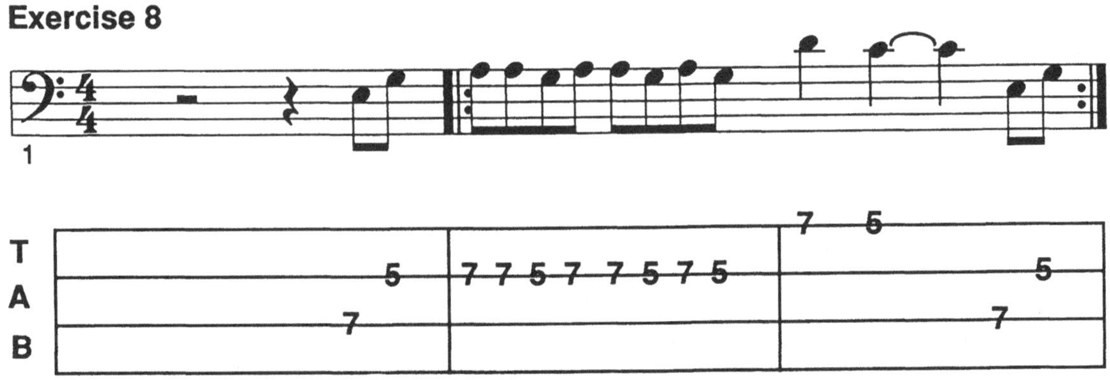

Scales

You've probably heard of scales before. They are the basis for all musical compositions. Scales determine all of the notes that can and will be played in a given piece of music. That doesn't mean that some notes from "outside" of the correct scale will not be used. But, for the most part, all notes in a piece of music come from the scale.

There is a structure that is used in music. It starts with something called the **KEY.** Remember the key signature? The key signature tells you what scale you will be playing in. A key is nothing more than a scale. Thus, the key signature tells you which key you will be playing in.

Chords are then constructed from the notes in the key (scale). And bass lines and melody lines are also constructed from the notes in the key, but they relate to the chord that is being played at that time. Got it? Okay, Beethoven, let's learn how to play a scale....

There are actually a number of different kinds of scales. We will be talking about major, minor, pentatonic, blues, and funk scales. First, the major scale....

There are two things to think about when constructing a major scale:

> **1. Start at the first note and play every note in the musical alphabet until the first note reappears.**
>
> **2. Each note in the scale must comply with the following series of intervals: W–W–H–W–W–W–H (where W = whole step; H = half step).**

Here's how to apply those two "rules." Let's talk about the C major scale. According to Rule #1 above, start at C and play every note in the musical alphabet until C reappears: C–D–E–F–G–A–B–C.

Now for Rule #2. Verify that the series of intervals between each note complies with the W–W–H–W–W–W–H pattern. That is, C–D should be a whole step, D–E should be a whole step, E–F should be a half step, etc.... If this is the case, then the notes C–D–E–F–G–A–B–C are the notes in the C major scale.

That one is simple. That's because **the C major scale is the only major scale with no sharps or flats.** That's right, the only one. Here's how to apply Rules #1 and #2 to other scales that do have sharps and flats:

Let's play a G major scale. Start at G and play all the way through the musical alphabet: G–A–B–C–D–E–F–G. Now apply the W–W–H–W–W–W–H pattern to those notes. Everything is hunky-dory until you reach the E–F interval. As we all know, E to F is only a half step. The major scale Rule #2 says it should be a whole step. What to do, what to do??? This is where sharps and flats come into play.

The W–W–H–W–W–W–H pattern must be followed. Therefore, the F is changed to an F♯. That makes it a whole step above the E and a half step below the G. Everybody's happy, right? Well, almost.... There are those who would argue that the F♯ could be called a G♭. Go back and look at Rule #1 again. Didn't I say that you have to have one of every note in the major scale? Yes, I did. Therefore, the note is an F♯, not a G♭.

The most important thing to remember about major scales is this pattern: W–W–H–W–W–W–H.

Let's play some scales now that we know a little about them.... Again, we will start with C major. We will first play it starting at the 3rd fret on the A-string. Then we will learn to play the C major scale in every position, all the way up the neck. Here's the C major scale:

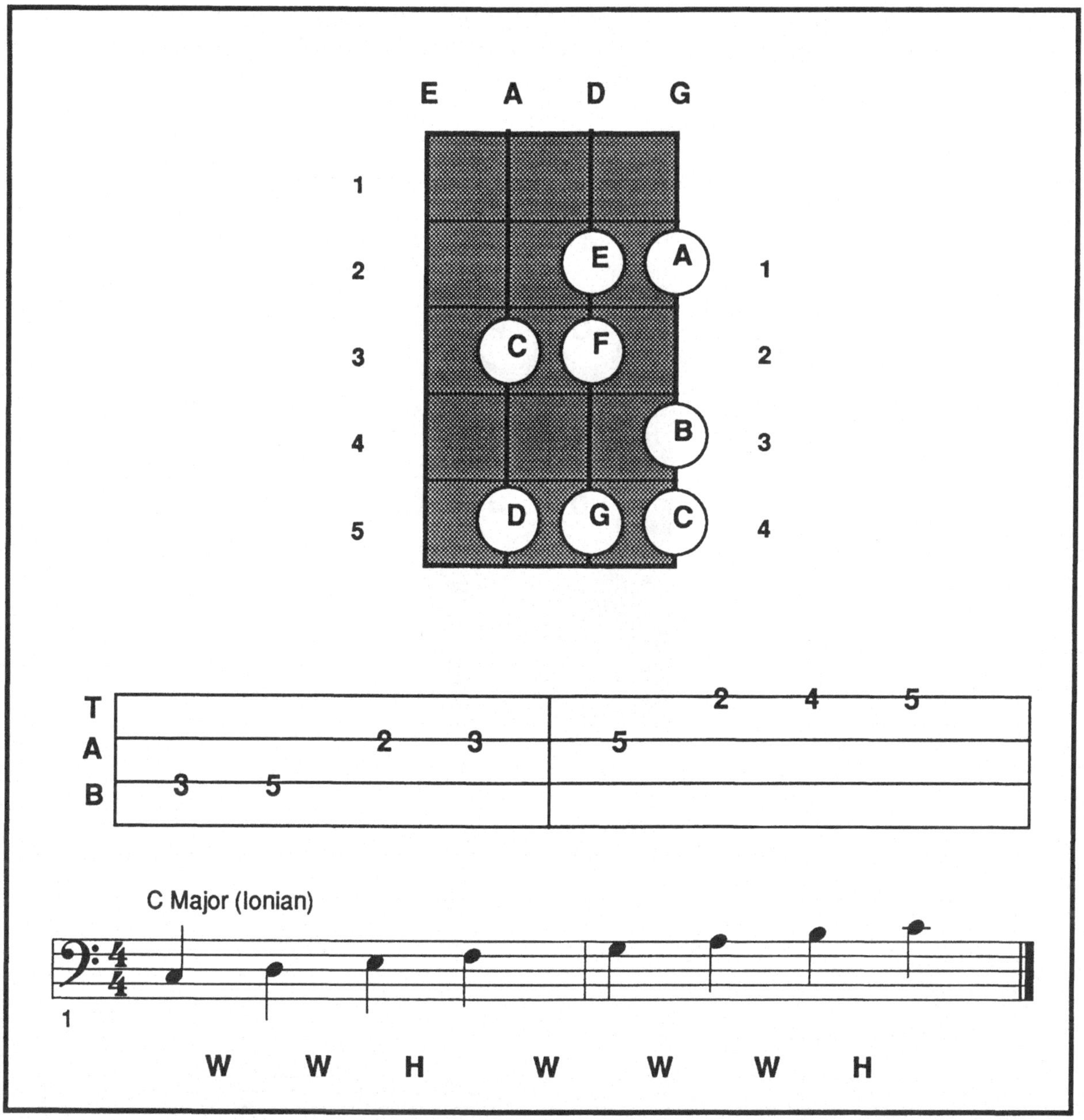

Memorize that pattern!!! This pattern can be moved to any location on the neck to play any other major scale. I know, you're thinking *"What???"* Hey, have I lied to you yet? Trust me....

Because of the relationship between the tuning of the strings on a bass, this pattern can be moved all over the neck. Pick any note anywhere on the neck. Place your second finger on that note. Now play the above pattern until you get to the eighth note in the pattern. You have just played the major scale for whatever that first note was!! If you started on an A, then it was an A major scale. If it was a D♭, then it was a D♭ major scale. You didn't know you knew so many scales, did you??

Okay, quit showing off and get back to the C major scale. If we move the E and A notes from the 2nd fret to the 7th fret, we get the exact same scale, played in a different position:

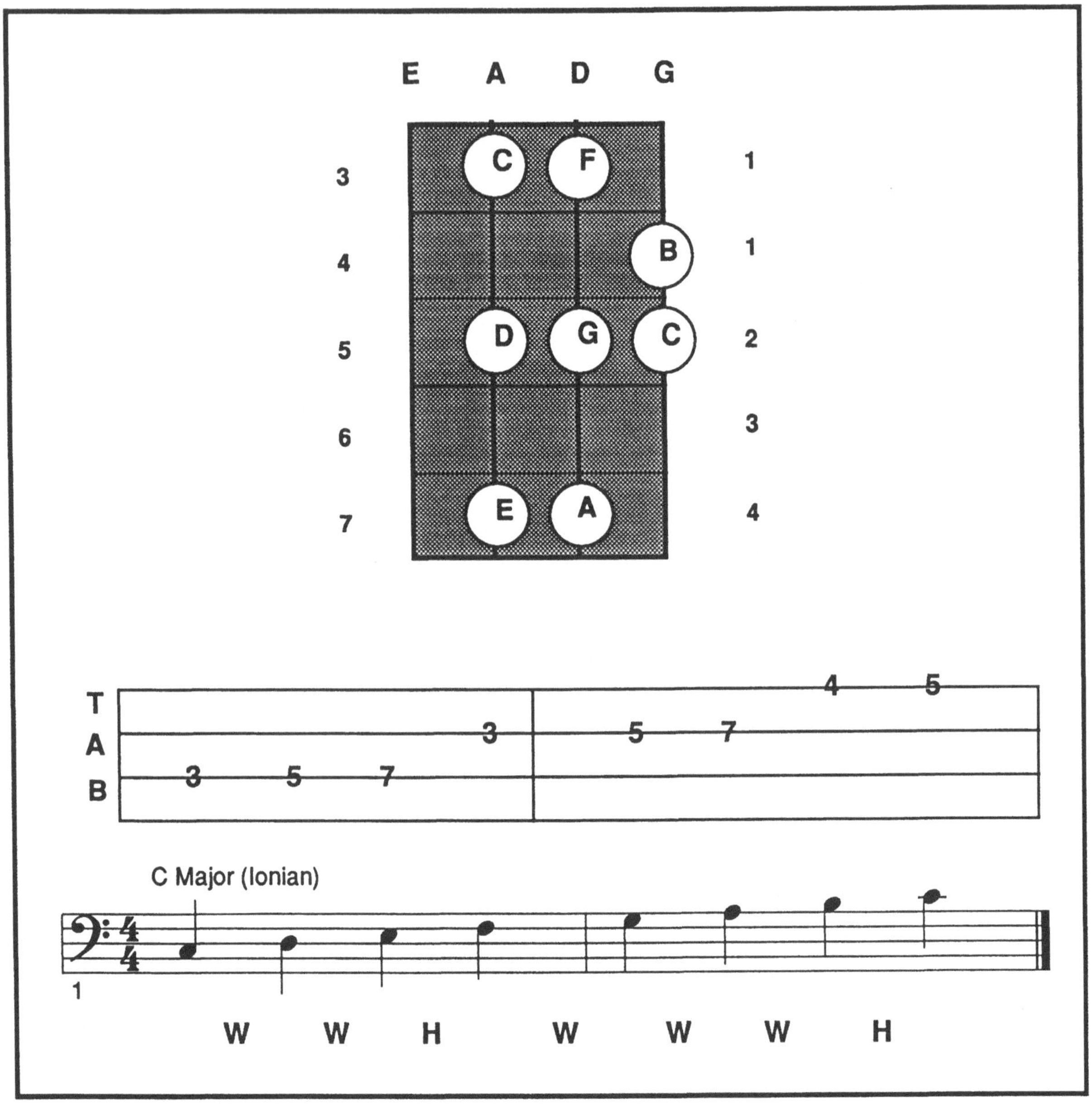

Now let's get a little more complicated! We are going to start the C major scale on a D note. That is called "starting from the 2nd" because D is the *second* note in the C major scale. The technical name for this type of scale is "D Dorian." That means to play a C major scale starting at the second note of the scale (in this case, D). D Dorian is what is called a **MODE.** There is a different mode for each note in a major scale. (When starting at the first note of the scale, the mode is called "Ionian.")

We will now look at the remaining modes and their patterns in C major. Learn each pattern really well. I recommend playing all seven modes in C major as an exercise each time you practice. Here we go....

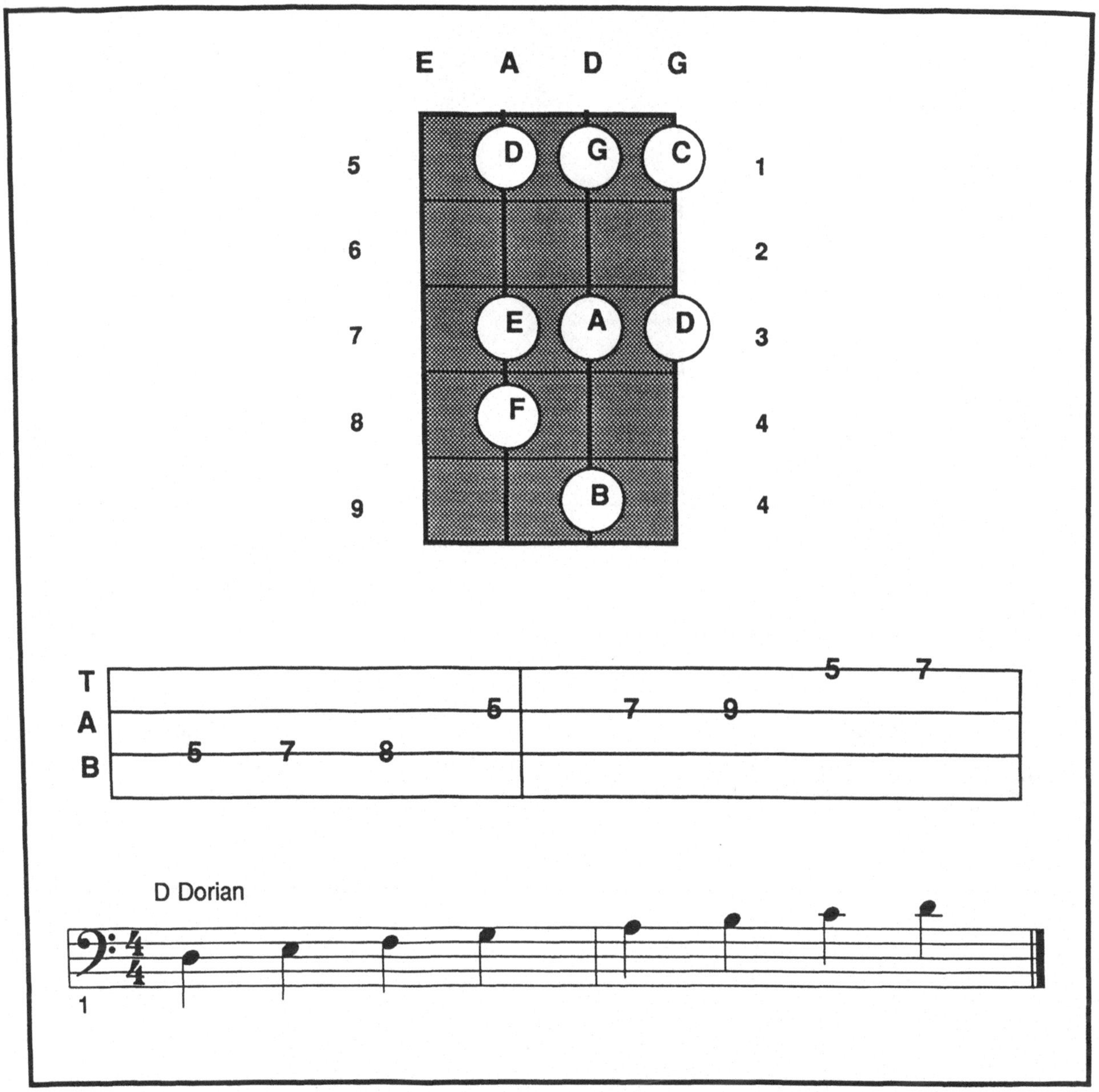

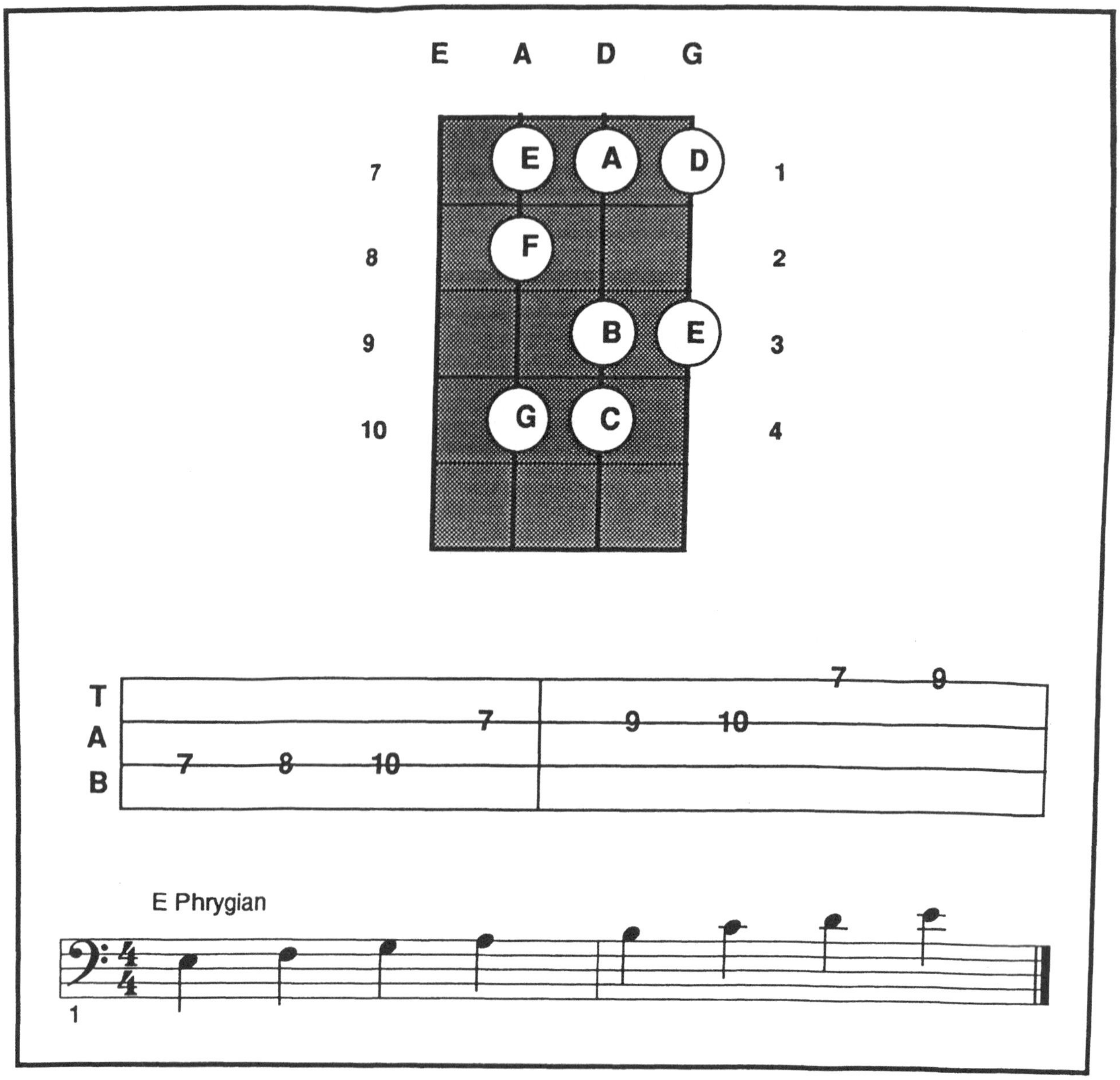
E A D G
7 E A D 1
8 F 2
9 B E 3
10 G C 4
T A B
7 8 10 7 9 10 7 9
E Phrygian
1

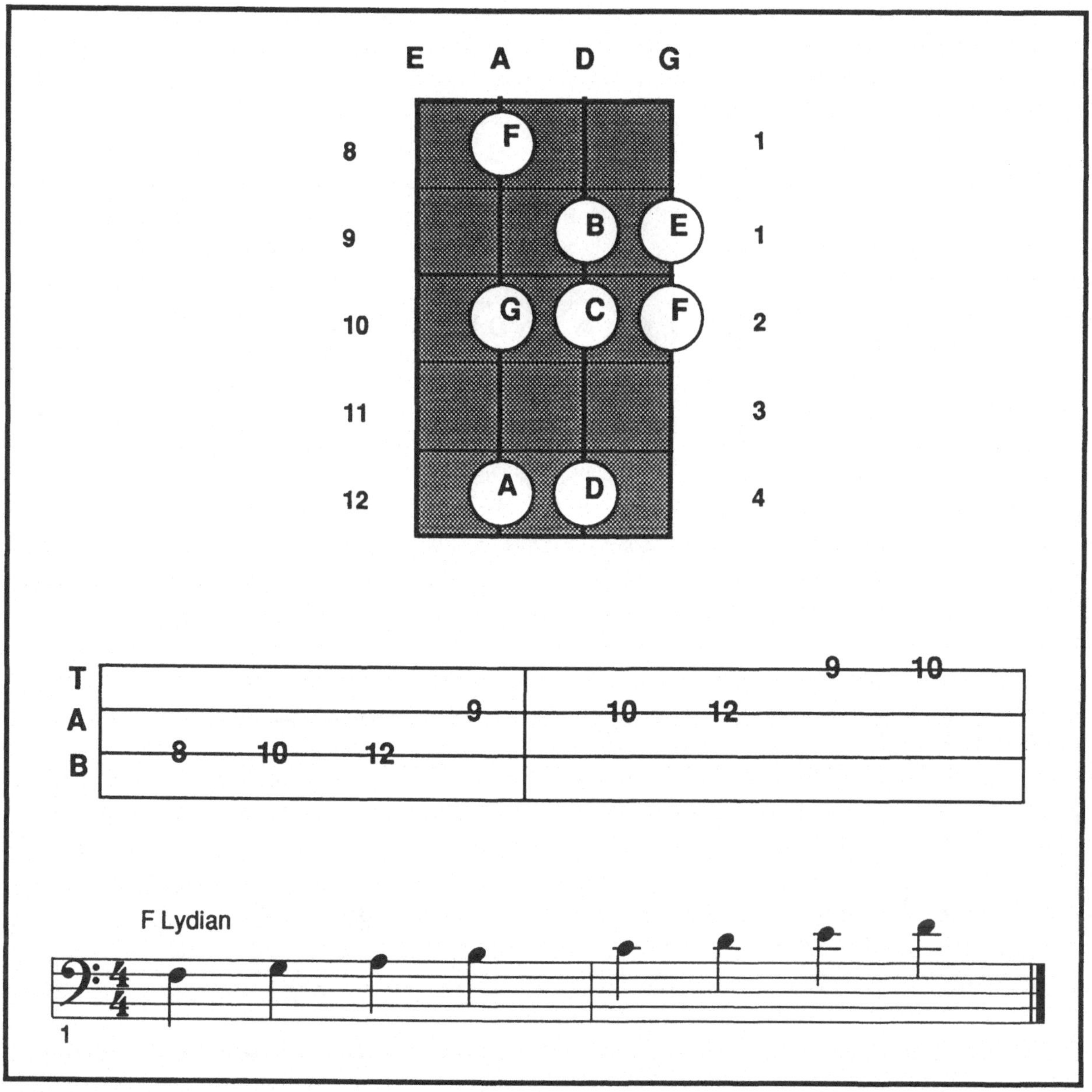
E A D G
8 9 10 11 12
1 1 2 3 4
F B E G C F A D
T
A
B
8 10 12 9 10 12 9 10
F Lydian

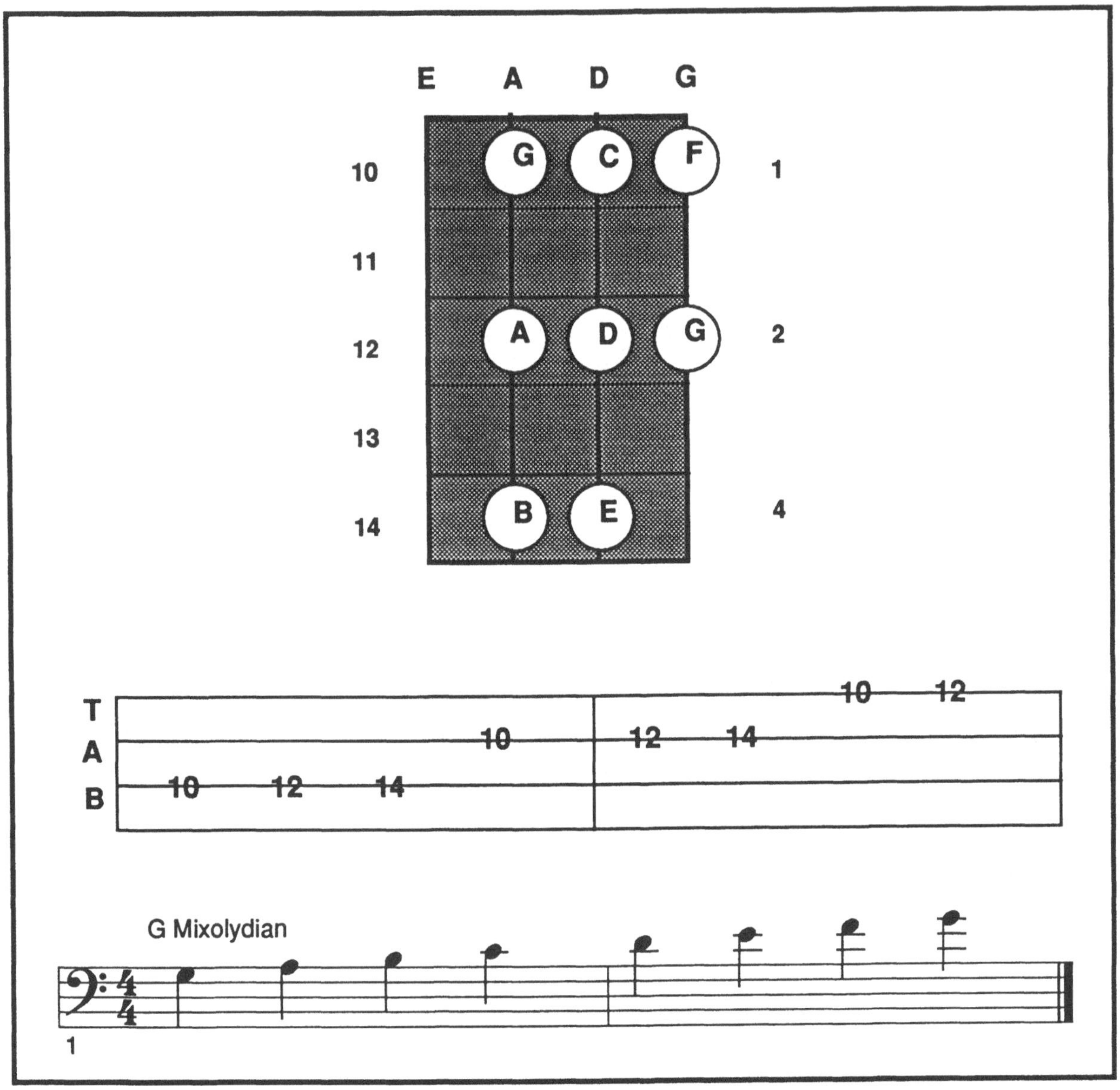
E A D G
10 G C F 1
11
12 A D G 2
13
14 B E 4
T
A
B
10 12 14 10 12 14 10 12
G Mixolydian
1

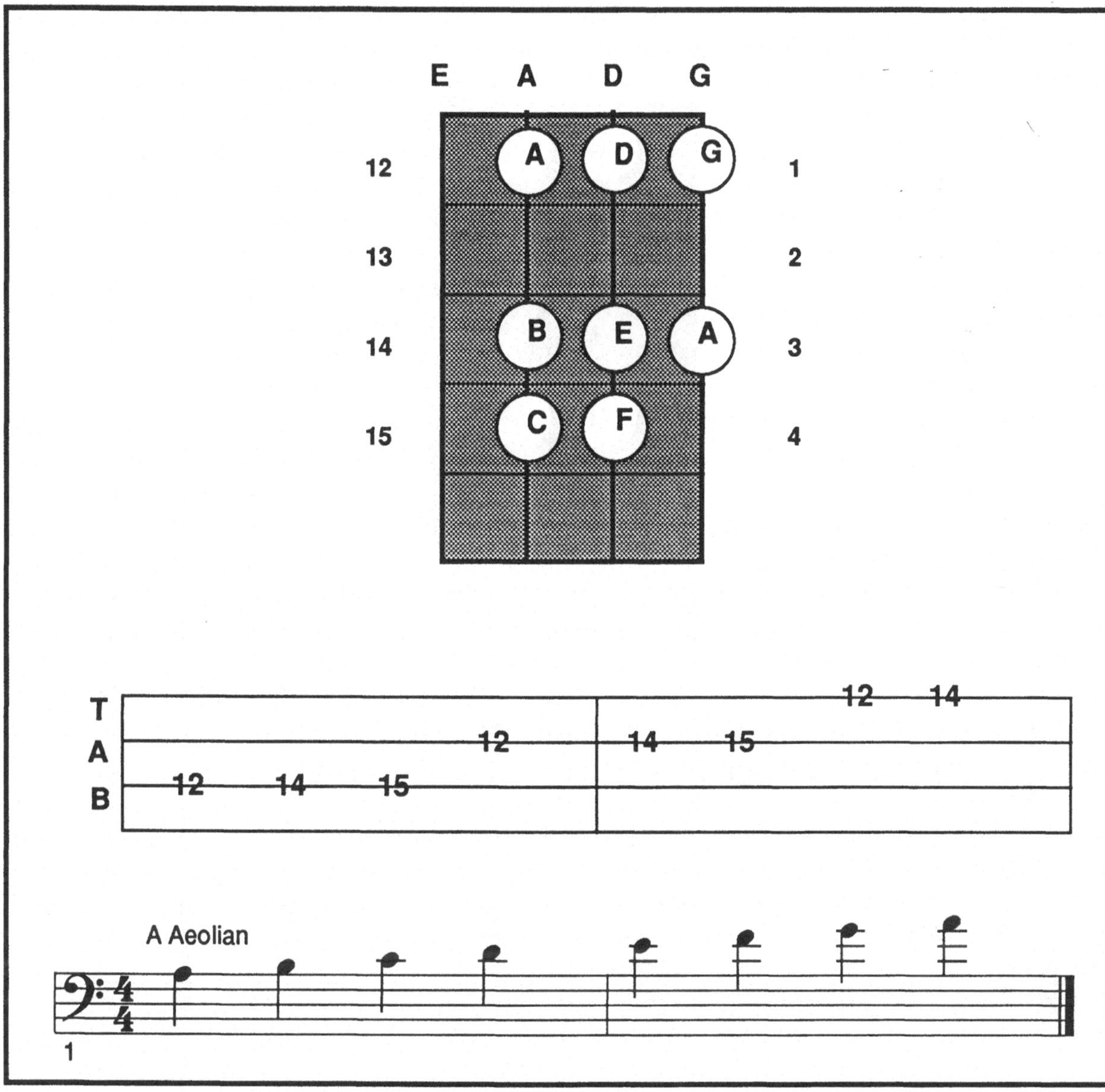
E A D G
12 A D G 1
13 2
14 B E A 3
15 C F 4
T
A
B
12 14 15 12 14 15 12 14
A Aeolian
1

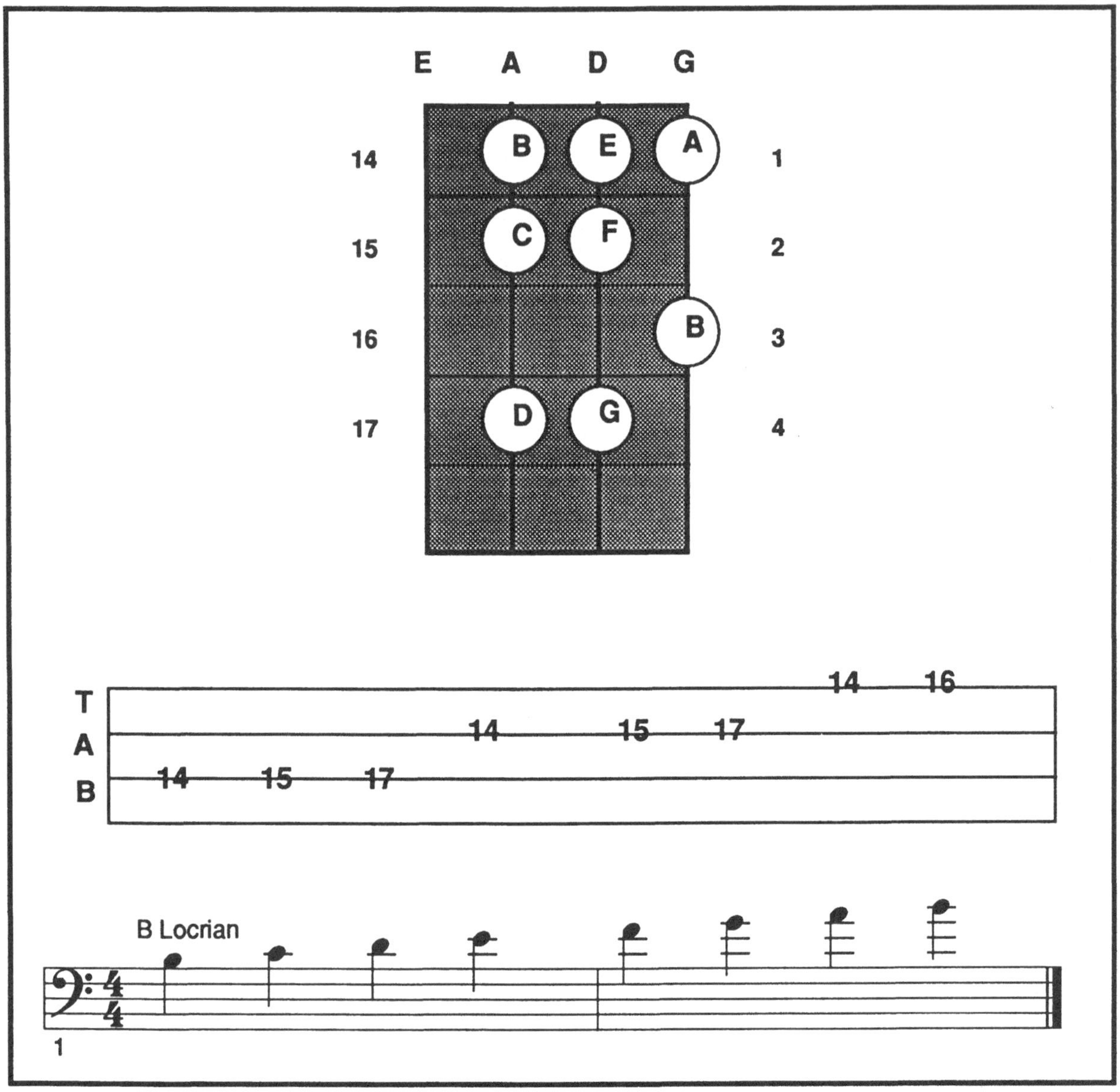
E A D G
14 B E A 1
15 C F 2
16 B 3
17 D G 4
T
A
B
14 15 17 14 15 17 14 16
B Locrian
1

Following are the rest of the major scales to be learned. After learning the scales in the basic pattern shown, go through and learn the modes for each scale. It is very important to have a very good grasp of all scale positions and patterns.

E Major

B Major

F♯ Major

F Major

B♭ Major

E♭ Major

Now let's talk a little about minor scales. Would you believe that you have already learned how to play minor scales? Well, you have!! There is a relationship between major and minor scales. To make it simple, the relationship is this: The sixth note of any major scale is also the first note (root) of its **RELATIVE MINOR SCALE.**

The details of this relationship are that the major scale has the *exact same notes* as the relative minor scale, starting at the sixth note of the major scale. Here's an example:

The C major scale consists of the notes C–D–E–F–G–A–B–C. The sixth note (A) is the first note (root) of the relative minor scale, A minor. The notes in the A minor scale are A–B–C–D–E–F–G–A. The same notes as C major, it just starts and ends at the sixth note (of the major scale).

Therefore, you already have played all 12 minor scales!! Let's play them some more. I'll get you started and then leave it to you to go through all 12 minor scales.

Play the A Aeolian scale that you learned earlier:

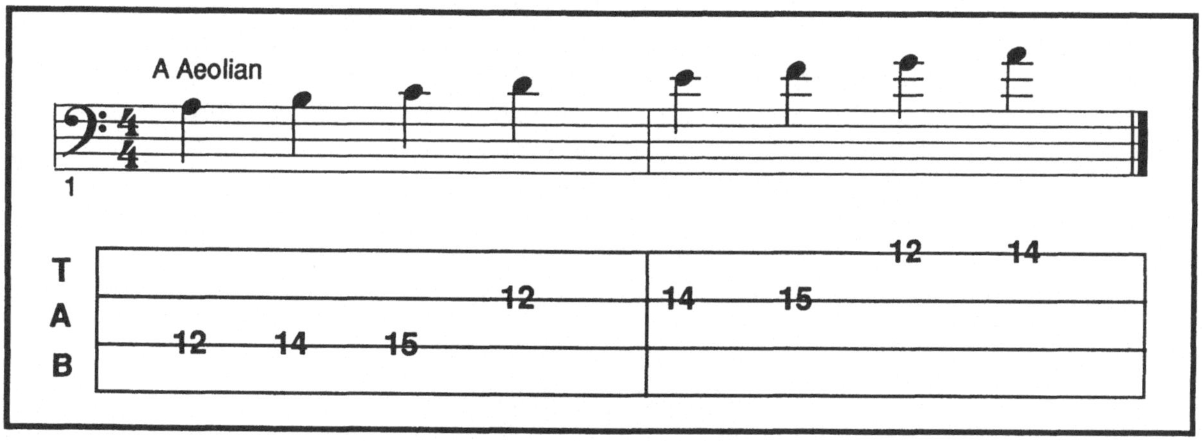

That is an A minor scale. Yes, it is the same as a C major scale starting at the sixth note. Let's drop it down an octave so we can learn it all the way up the neck:

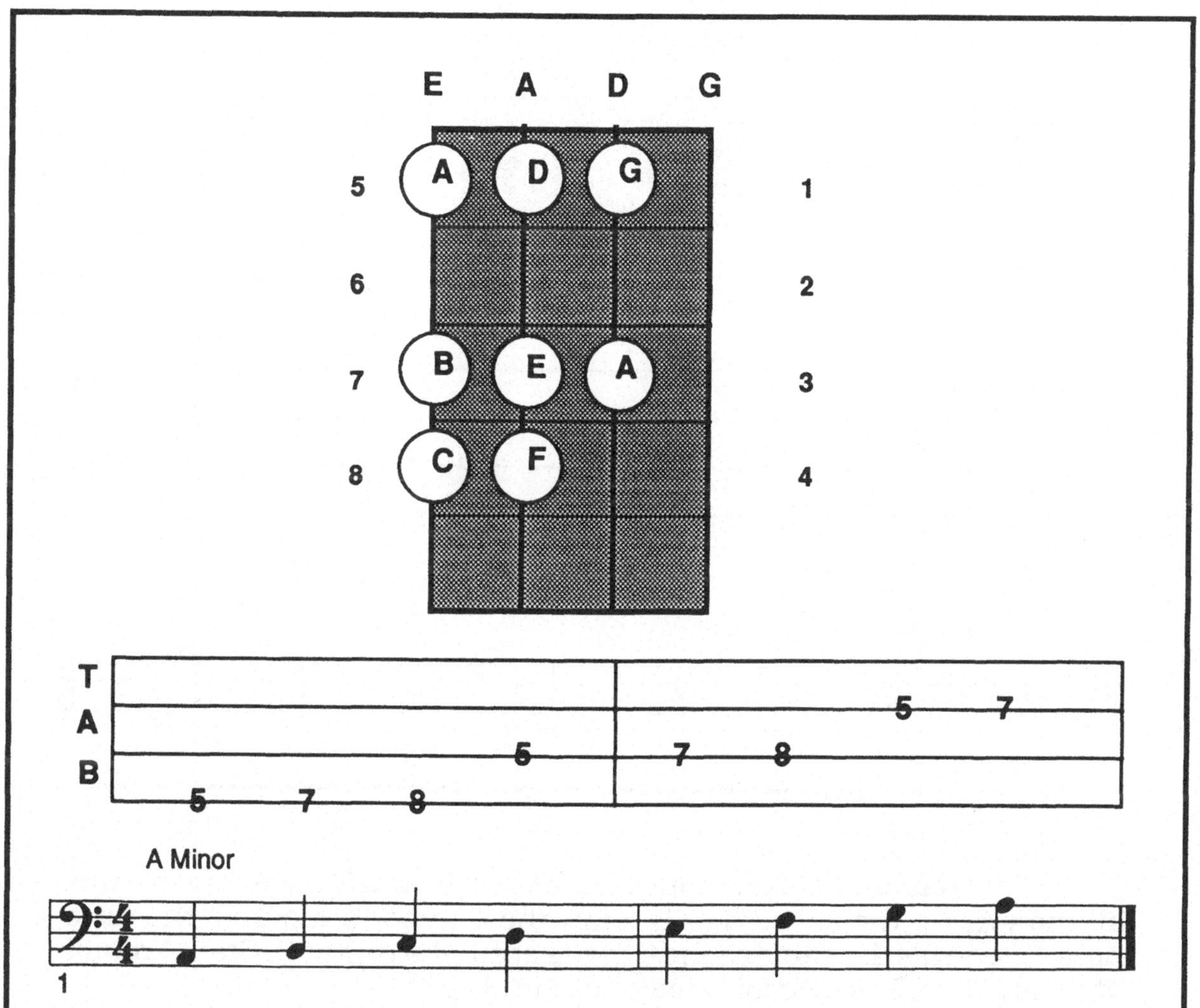

Now we'll try not to get too confusing, but follow me on this one....

If the A minor scale, starting at the root (A), is played exactly the same way as the A Aeolian scale and has the same notes as the C major scale, then the A minor scale starting at the second note in the scale (B) must be the same as the B Locrian scale (C major starting at the seventh note in the C major scale). Follow that?? Look at this diagram and compare it to the B Locrian scale shown earlier. They are the same, except this one is just played an octave lower.

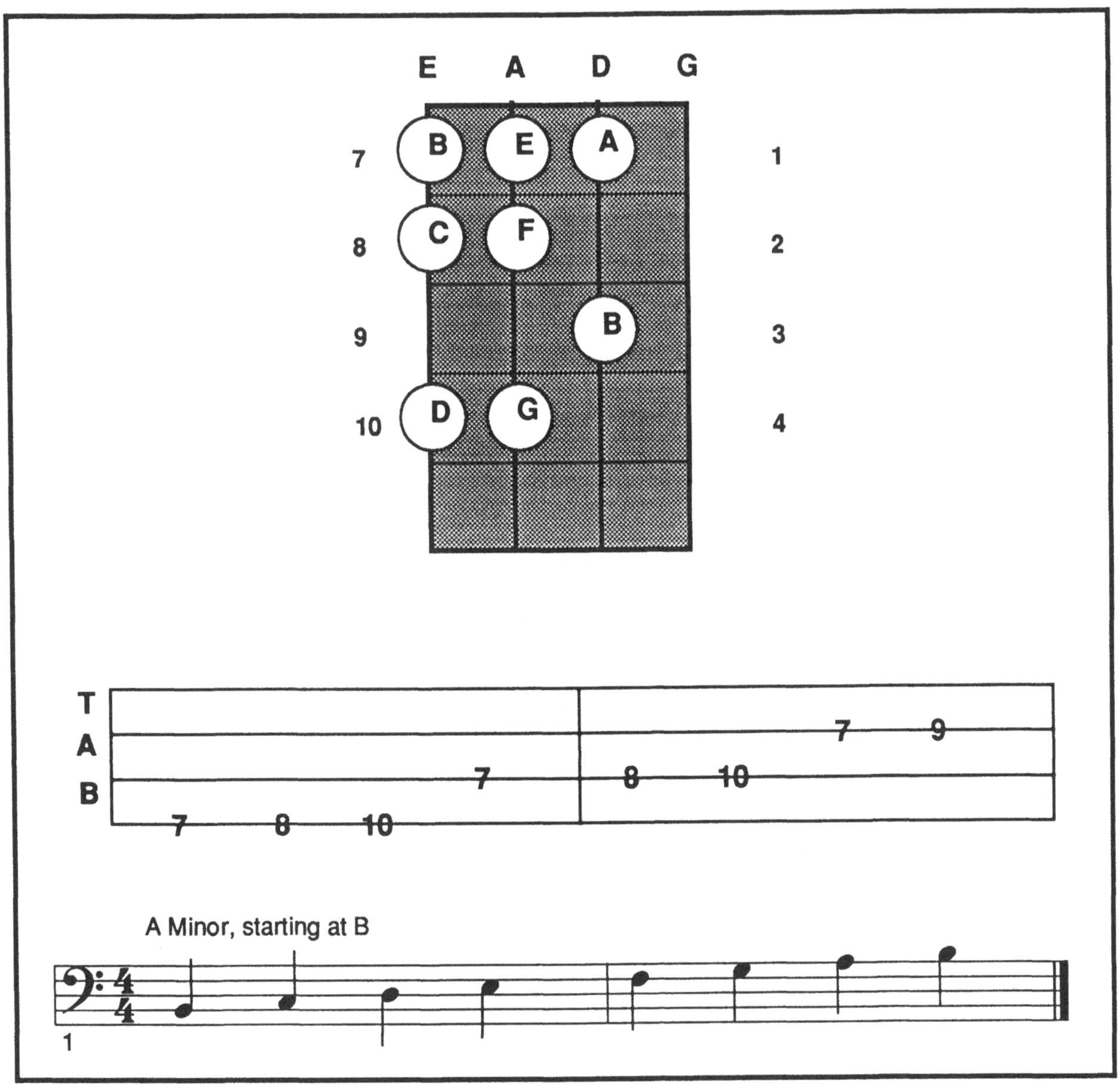

This relationship continues all the way through the A minor scale, all the way up the neck. That is, start the A minor scale from the third note, C, and it's the same as the C major scale starting at C. Start A minor at D, and it's the same as C major starting at D.

By the way, the mode names for the different versions of scale do not change from major to minor. In other words, A minor starting at B is still called "B Locrian." Starting at C, it's called "C Ionian," etc....

Now it's time for you to go off and learn all 12 of the minor scales all the way up the neck. Here's a chart of major scales and their relative minor scales:

Major	Relative Minor
C Major	A Minor
G Major	E Minor
D Major	B Minor
A Major	F♯ Minor
E Major	C♯ Minor
B Major	G♯ Minor
F♯ Major	D♯ Minor
F Major	D Minor
B♭ Major	G Minor
E♭ Major	C Minor
A♭ Major	F Minor
D♭ Major	B♭ Minor

More Scale Stuff . . . .

You didn't think we were through with this scale stuff yet, did you?? No, no, no.... I said it was the basis for everything!!

Actually, the rest of the scales we are going to talk about are variations on the major and minor scales you have already learned. They can each be applied to specific styles of music, as well. Let's get into it!!

MINOR PENTATONIC SCALES are five-note versions of a natural minor scale. Minor pentatonic scales are used frequently in rock, heavy metal, blues, and funk.

A minor pentatonic scale is the first, third, fourth, fifth, and seventh tones of the minor scale. Therefore, the A minor pentatonic is A–C–D–E–G. Here's what it looks like:

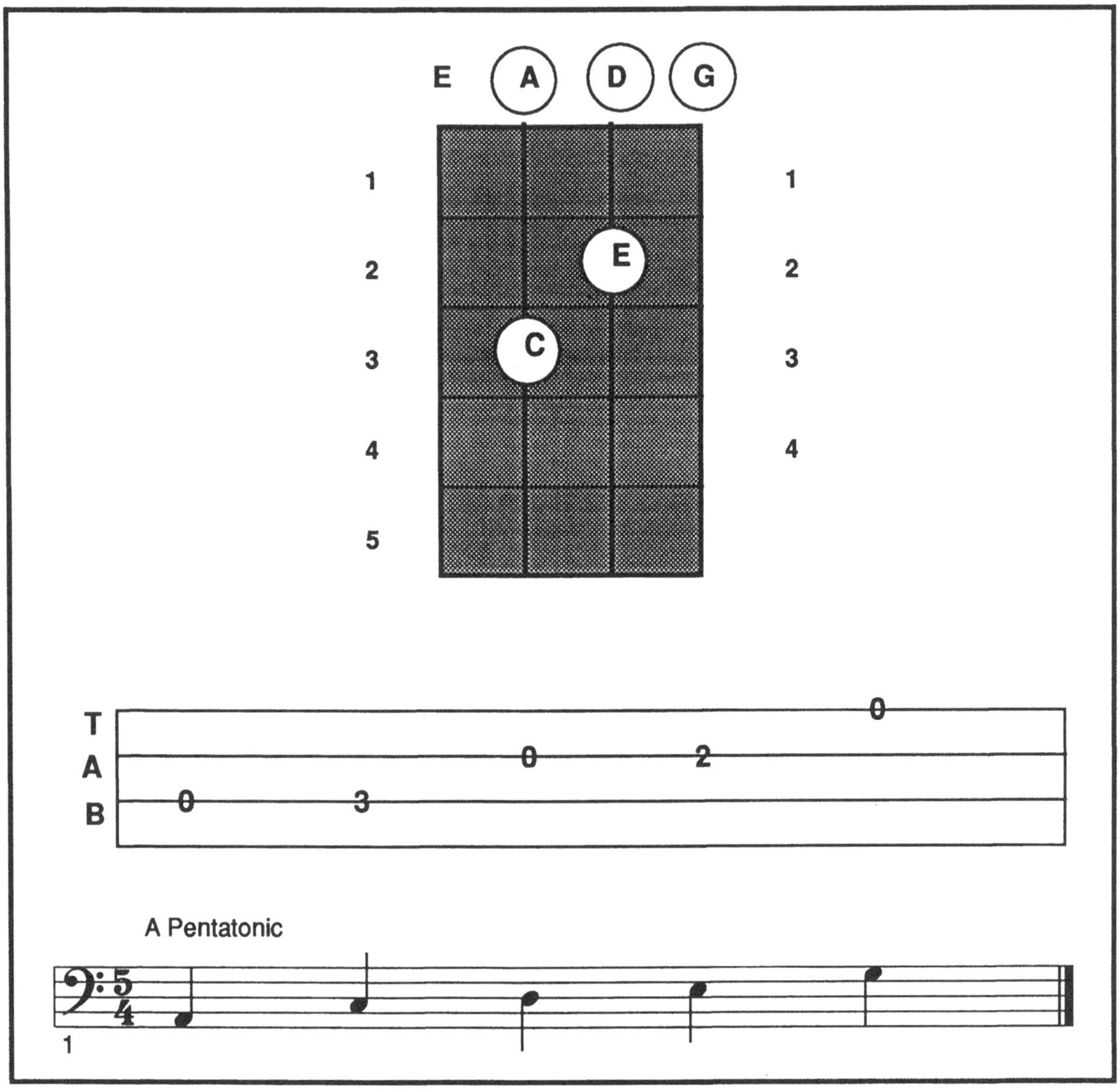

Like the major and minor scales, minor pentatonic scales can be expanded and played all over the neck. Here are all of the positions for the A minor pentatonic scale. Notice that, in these examples, we are playing the scale on all four strings. We are not adding any new notes, just playing each note in every possible location within a position. The patterns would be the same for any other minor pentatonic scale. So, once you get the A minor pentatonic patterns down, try some other keys, as well!!

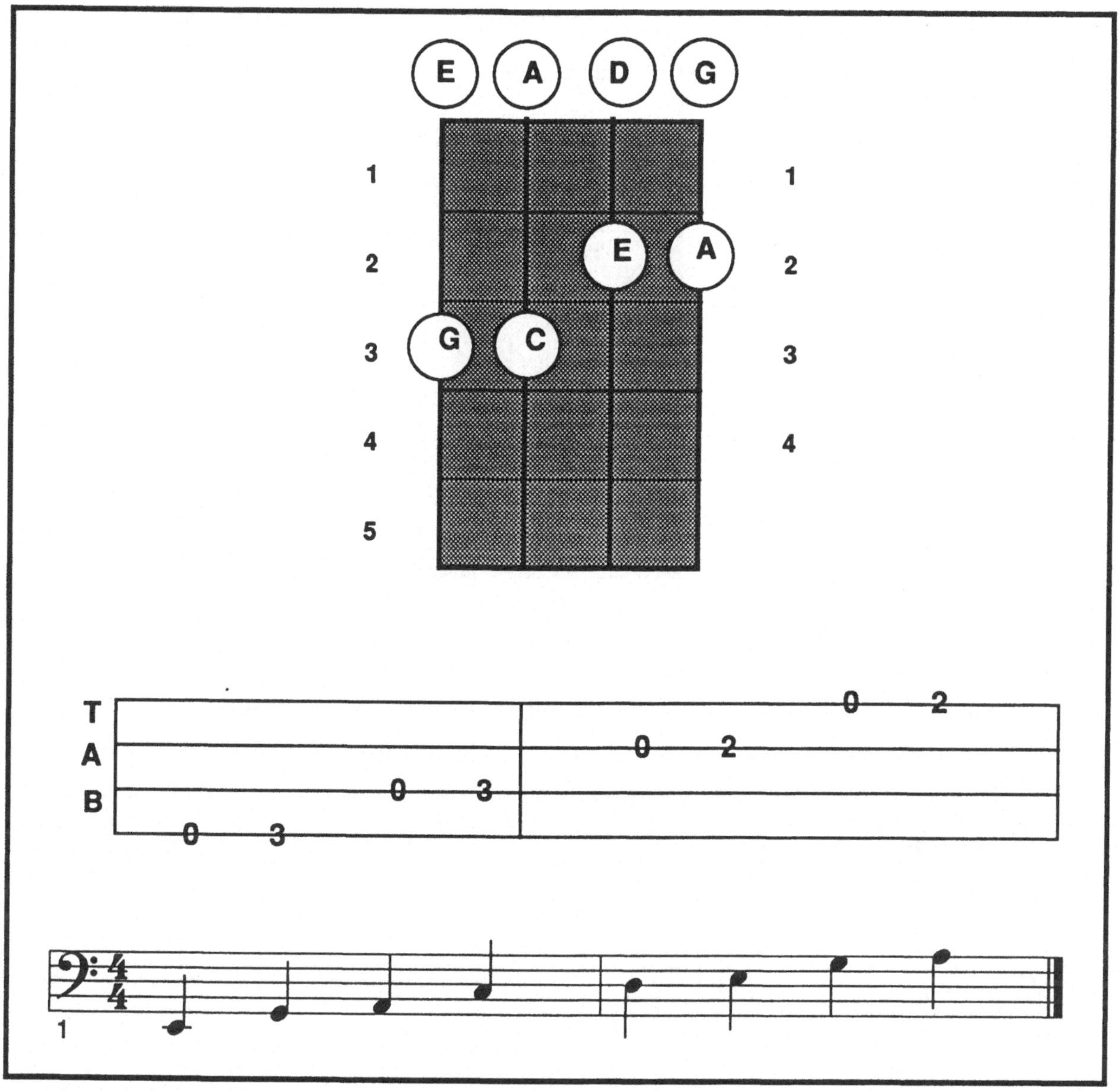
E A D G
1 2 3 4 5
E A G C
T A B
0 3 0 3 0 2 0 2
1

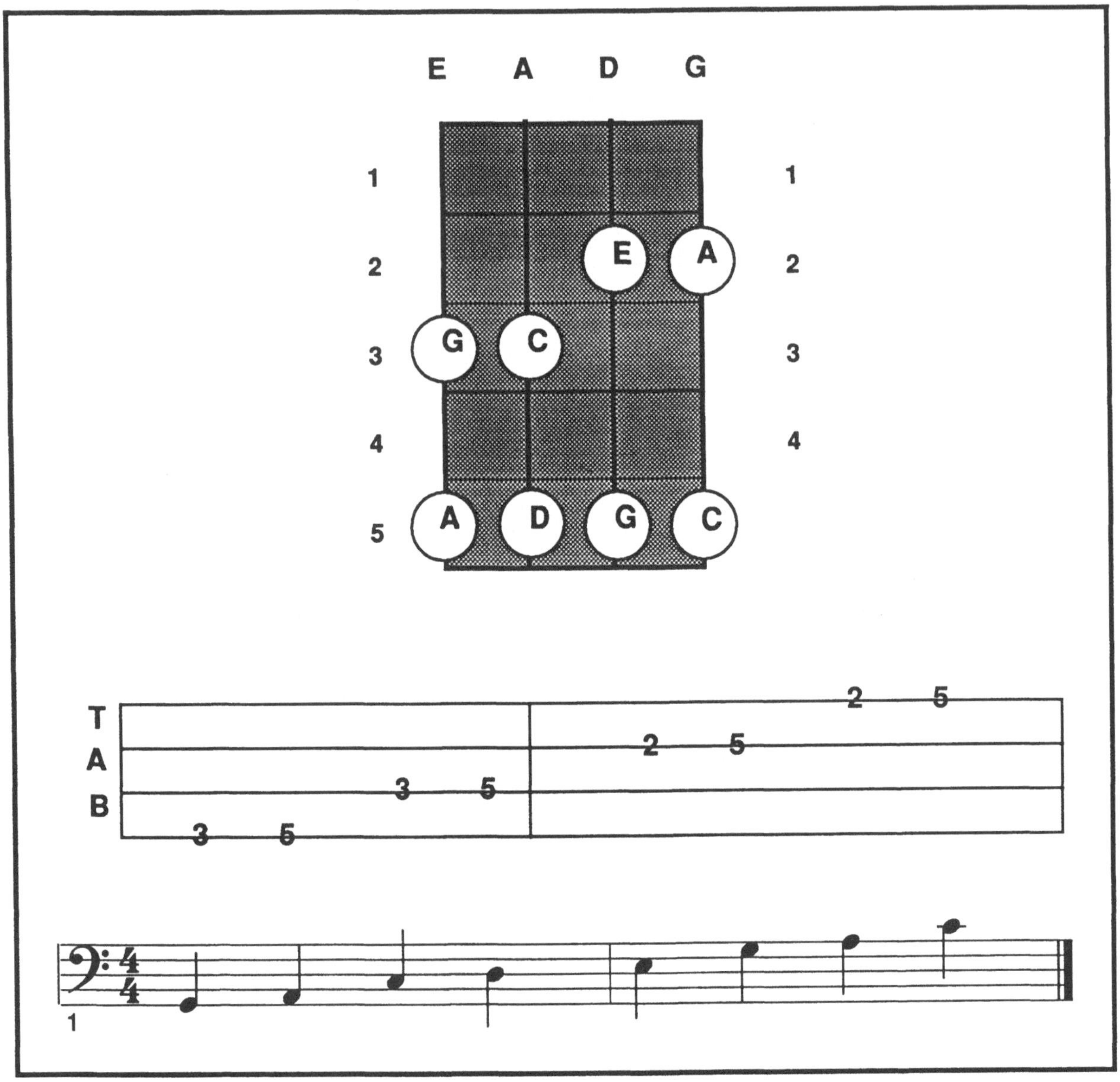

E A D G
1 1
2 2
3 3
4 4
5
E A
G C
A D G C
T
A
B
3 5 3 5 2 5 2 5
1

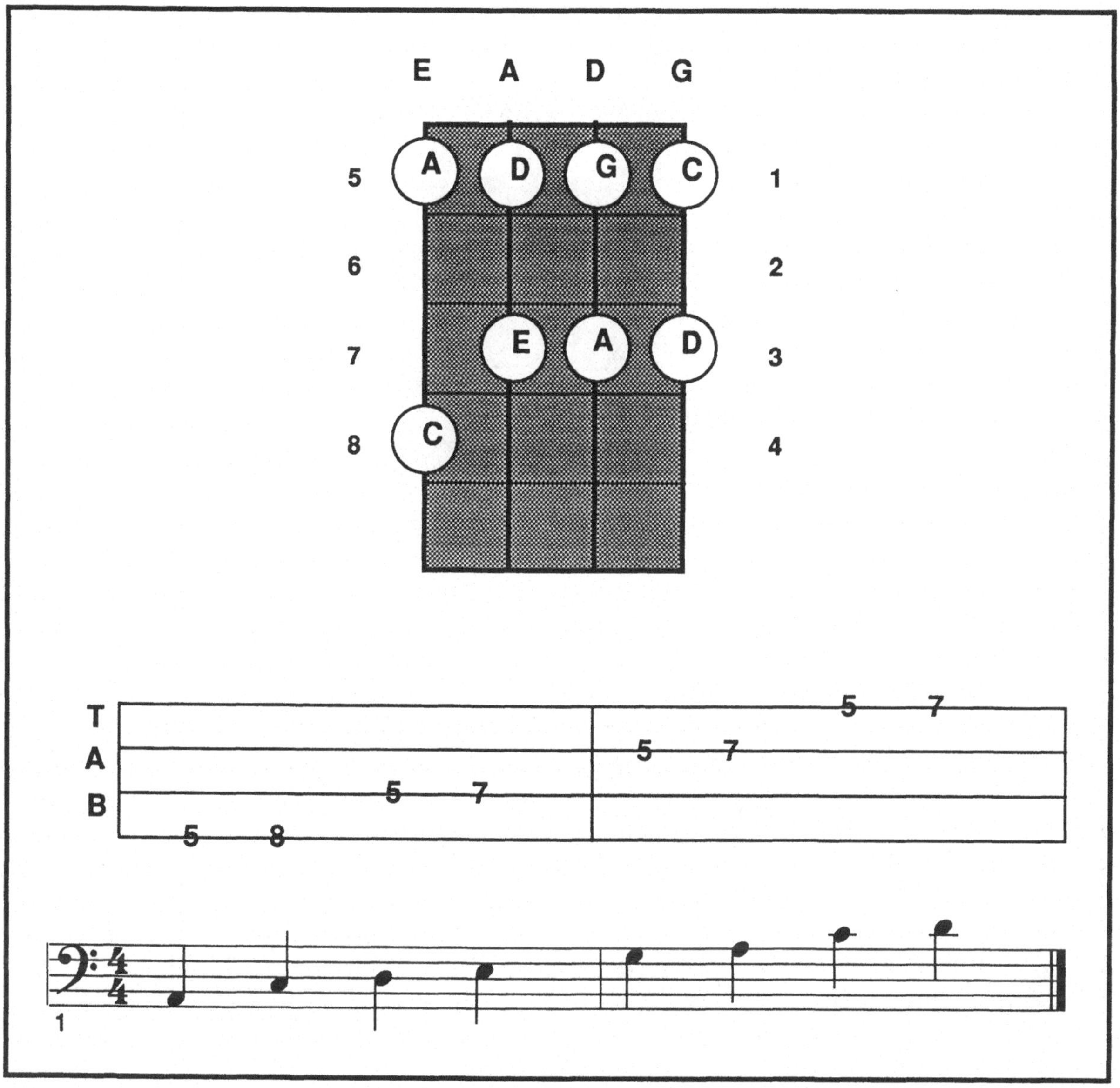
E A D G
A D G C
E A D
C
5
6
7
8
1
2
3
4
T
A
B
5 8 5 7 5 7 5 7
1

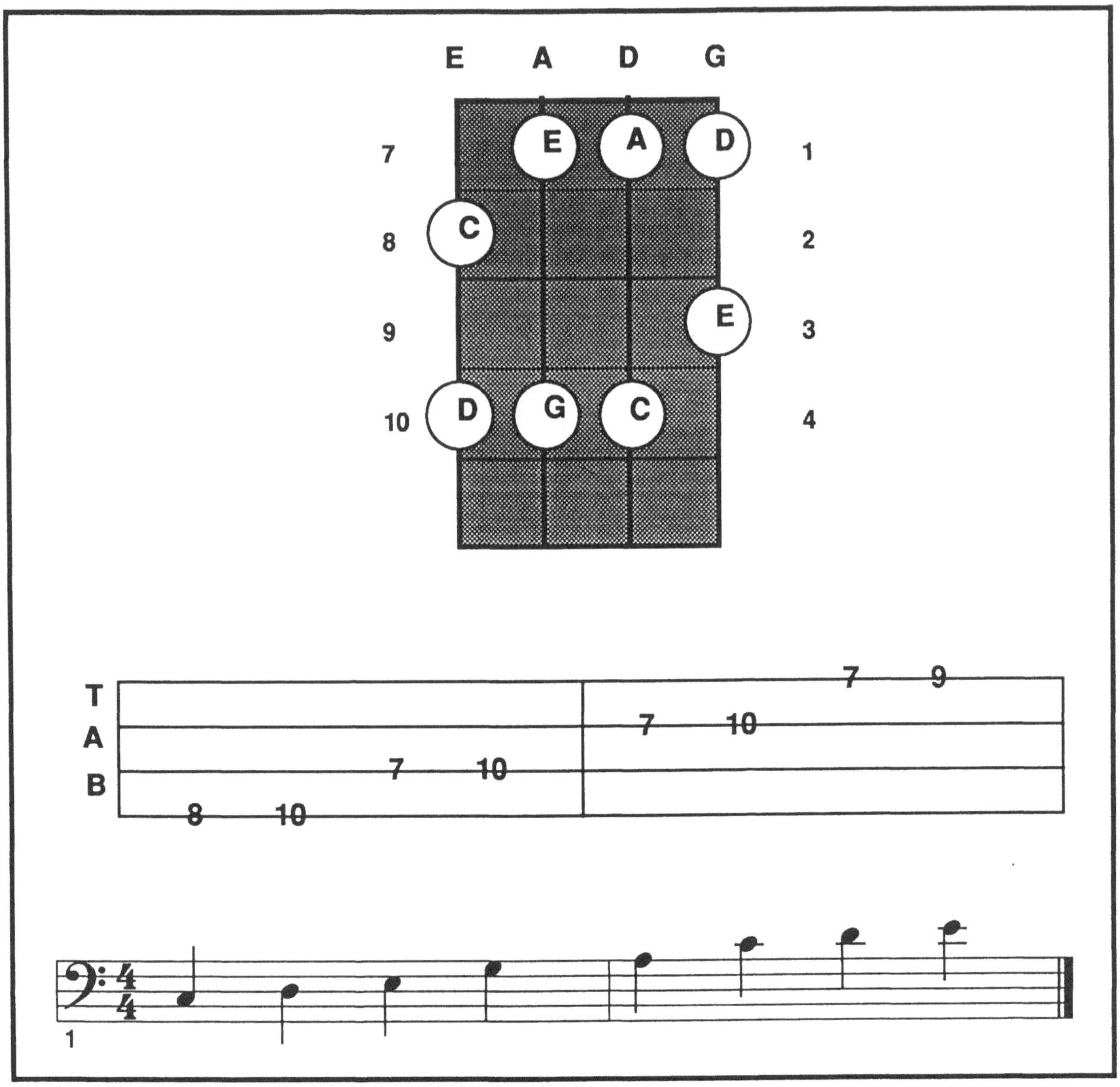
E A D G
7 E A D 1
8 C 2
9 E 3
10 D G C 4
T
A
B
8 10 7 10 7 10 7 9
1

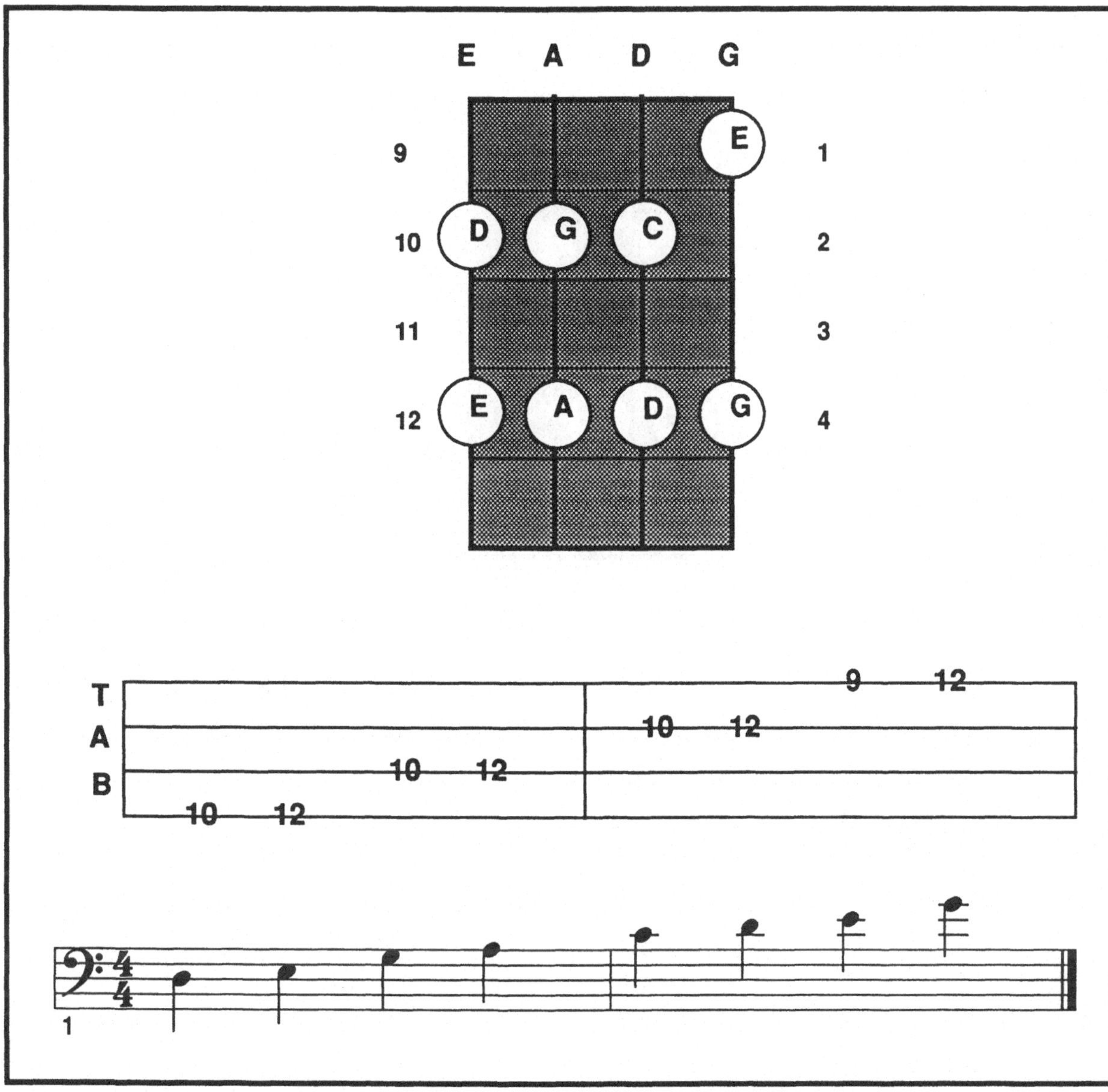
E A D G
9 E 1
10 D G C 2
11 3
12 E A D G 4
T
A
B
10 12 10 12 10 12 9 12
1

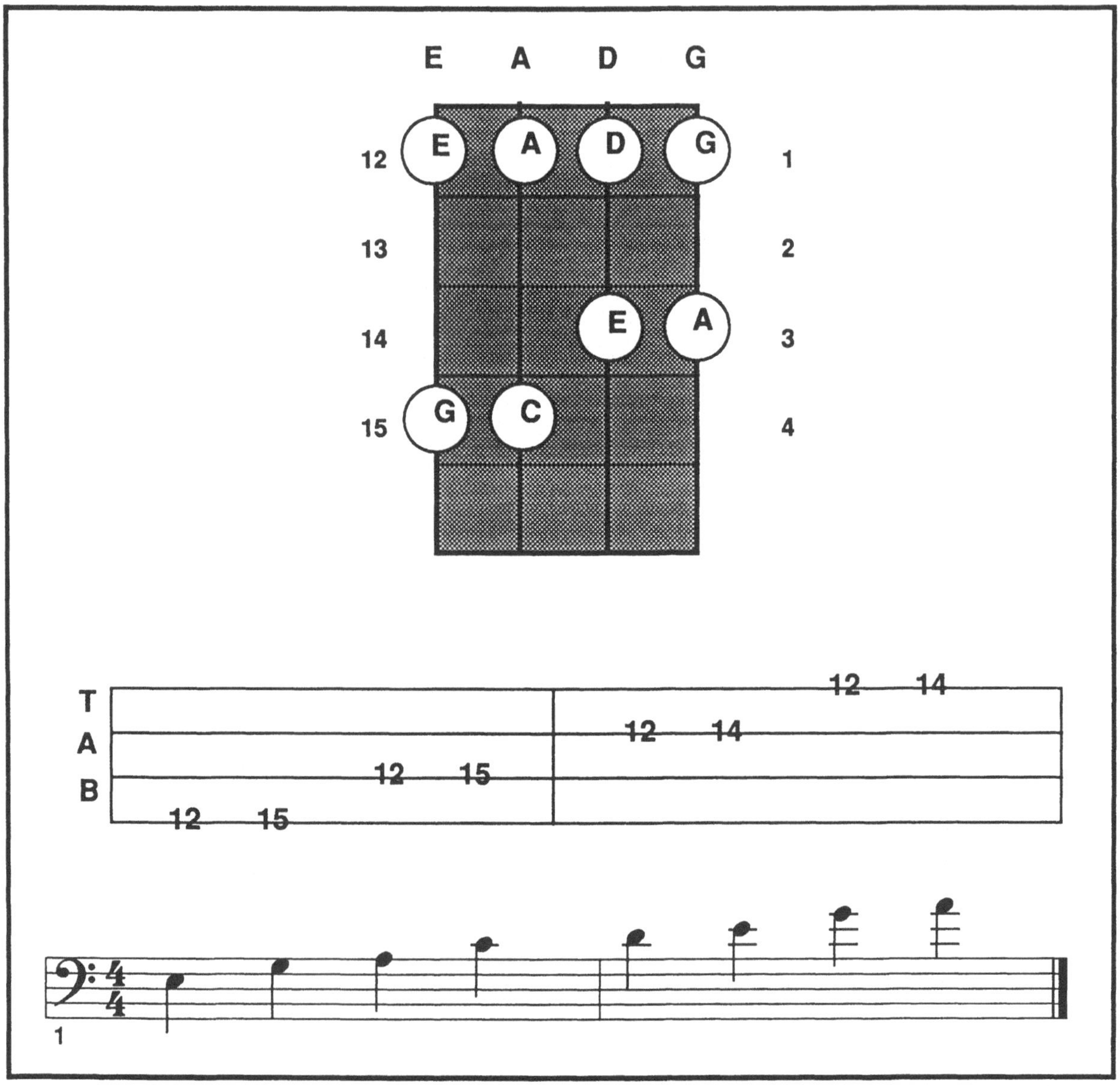
E A D G
12 E A D G 1
13 2
14 E A 3
15 G C 4
T
A
B
12 15 12 15 12 14 12 14
1

Here are a couple of minor pentatonic lines to work on. They are similar, but it is useful to be able to play each one cleanly and easily. Make up some of your own variations on these patterns to develop some more minor pentatonic lines and fills!

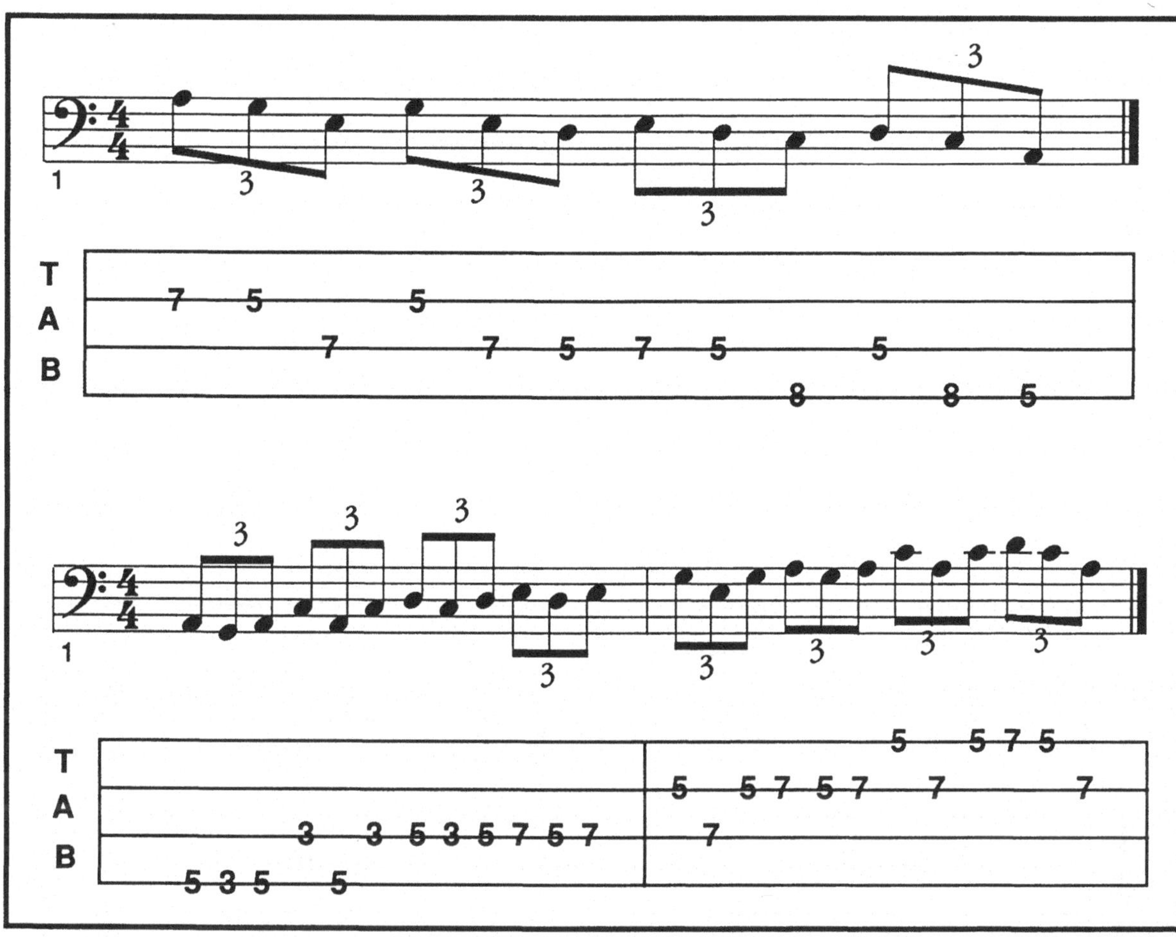

A blues scale is the same as a minor pentatonic scale with the addition of the flatted 5th of the scale. A flat 5, as it is often called, is simply the note that is one half step below the fifth note in the major or minor scale. In the A minor pentatonic scale, the 5th is the note E. Thus, the flat 5 is the note E♭.

Here is the A blues scale. As with every other scale, the blues scale can be played all up and down the neck. From now on, I'm going to leave it to you to expand the scales over the full length of the neck.

Here's an example of how a blues scale may be used in a bass line:

It is very common to add one more note to the blues scale. That note is the major 3rd. The blues scale uses the third note from the minor scale. In addition to that, we will often use the major 3rd, or the third note from the same major scale. Here is the A blues scale with the major 3rd note added. The C♯ note comes from the A major scale, where C♯ is the third note in that scale.

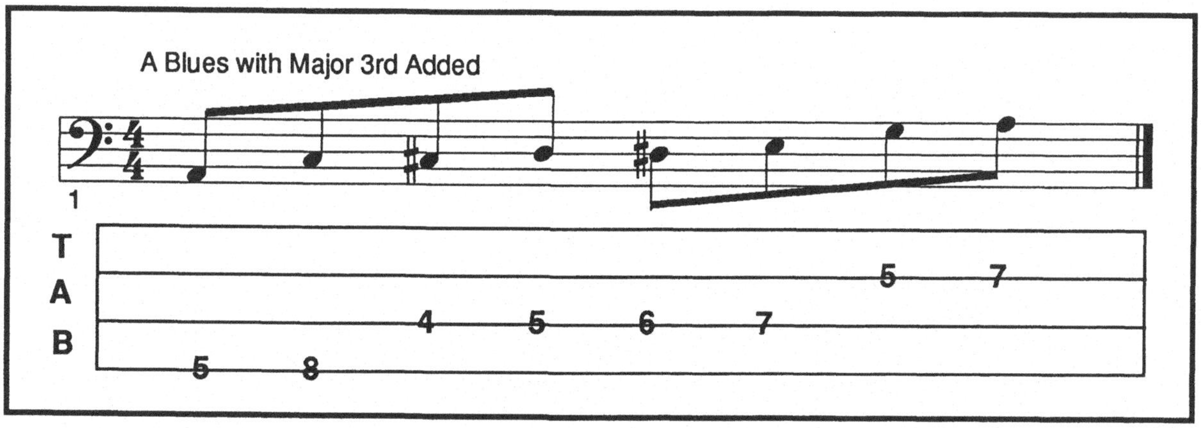

Here's a sample line that uses the A blues scale with the major 3rd added in. These kinds of ideas are very useful in many rock and blues styles of bass playing.

A funk scale is actually the same as the Mixolydian mode in a major scale. It is a major scale played with a flatted 7th note. (NOTE: A flatted 7th is also called a "dominant 7th.") Let's take a look at an E funk scale. It consists of the notes E–F♯–G♯–A–B–C♯–D–E. All the notes are the same as the E major scale, except for the 7th note, which is a D♮ instead of a D♯. That D is the dominant 7th. Here's what it looks like:

Here are a couple of typical funk lines in E. Play them over and over, and then start playing with some variations on each pattern using other notes from the E funk scale shown above.

It is very common to add a minor 3rd note into the usual funk scale. If we do this to the E funk scale, it would look like this:

Here are some examples using the major 3rd mixed in with the E funk scale:

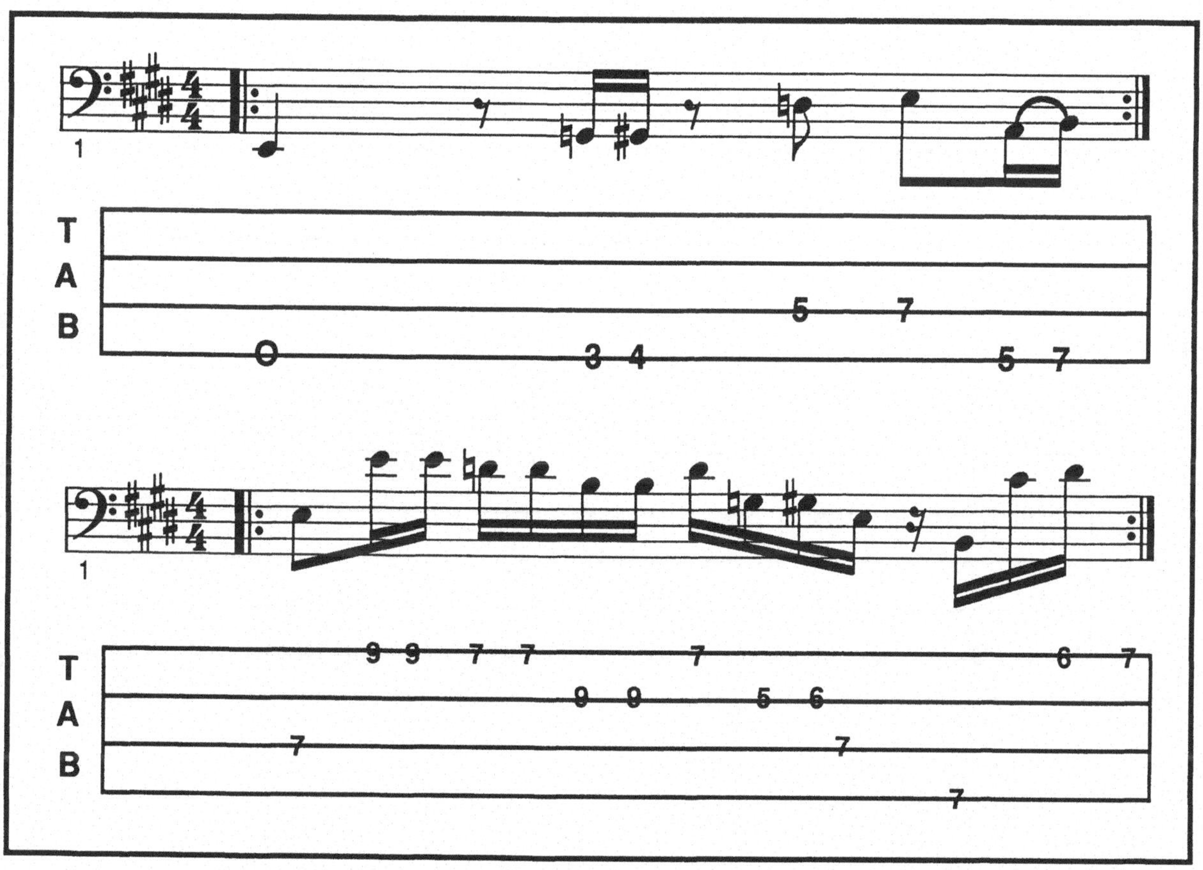

Bass Lines and Fills

Here are some examples of typical rock, pop, reggae, blues, and funk bass lines and fills. The best thing that you can do for yourself is to learn each line and fill and analyze each one to see which note of the scale you are using. This will help you understand the construction of bass lines and fills. Then you will have the necessary tools to go off and create your own lines and fills!

Above each piece of music are some possible chords that could be played during the bass line or fill ("A/A7" means A major or A 7th chords could be played). We'll start with bass lines that could be played against major chords.

Example 1

Example 2

Example 3

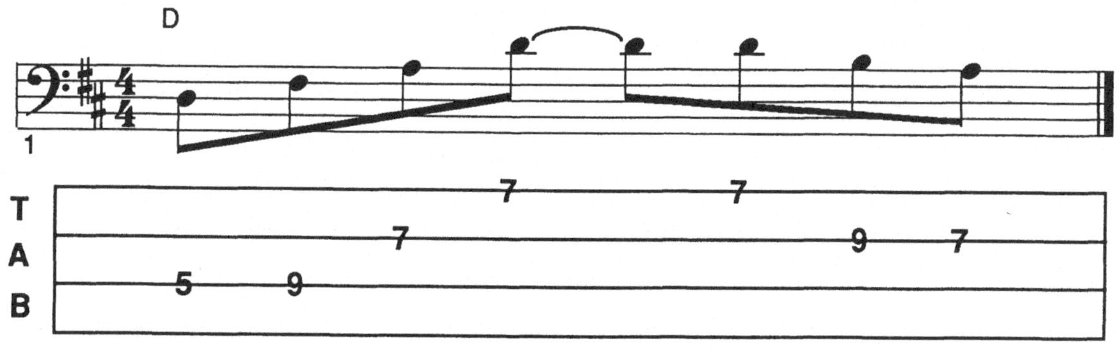

Example 4

Example 5

Example 6

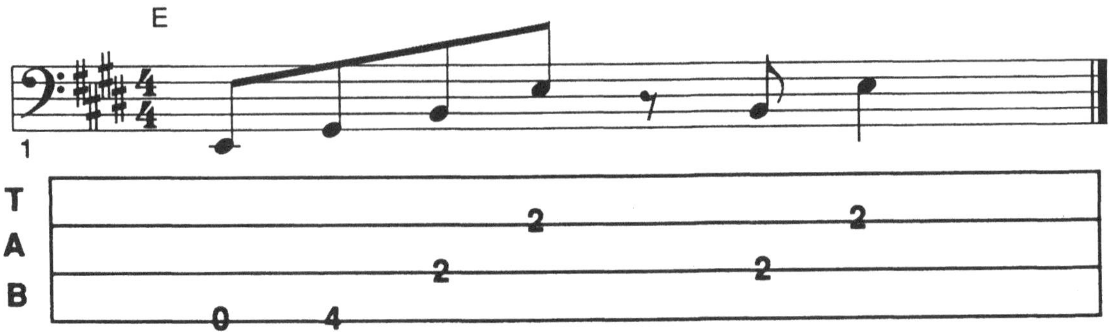

Example 7

Example 8

Example 9

Example 10

Example 11

Now we'll look at some bass lines that could be played against minor chords. Notice that some of them are very similar to some of the previous major-chord bass lines, the difference being that we are playing minor 3rds instead of major 3rds! This is useful to know, as you can adapt bass lines from other major chords to minor chords and vice versa.

Example 12

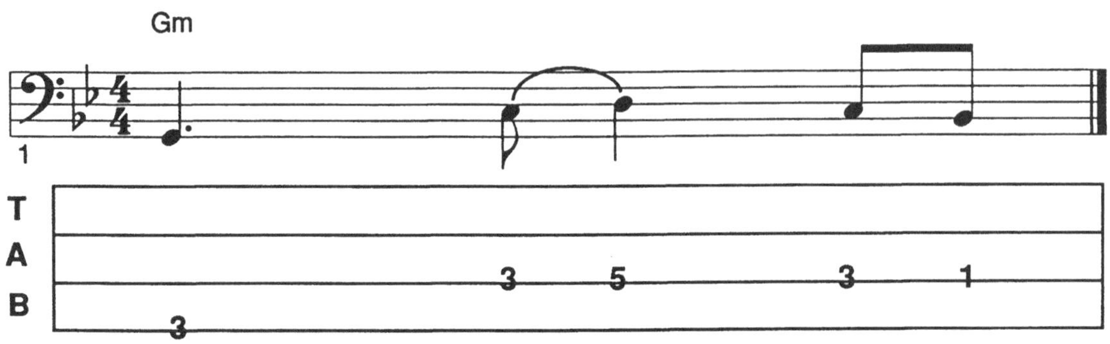

Example 13

Example 14

Example 15

Example 16

Example 17

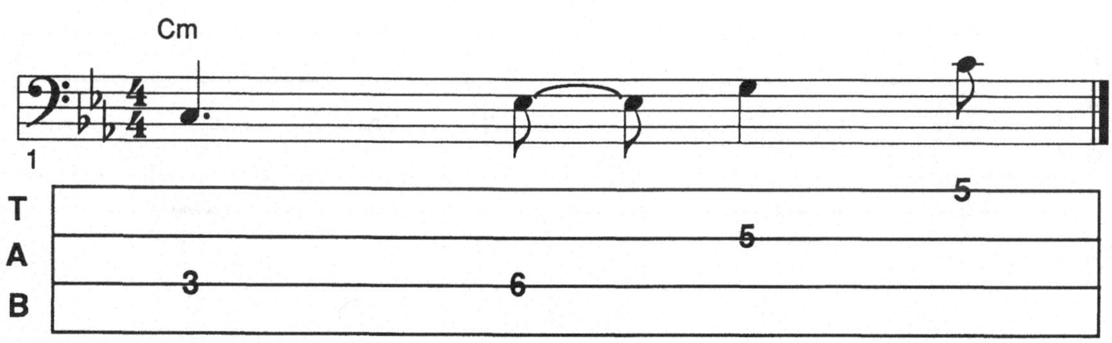

Example 18

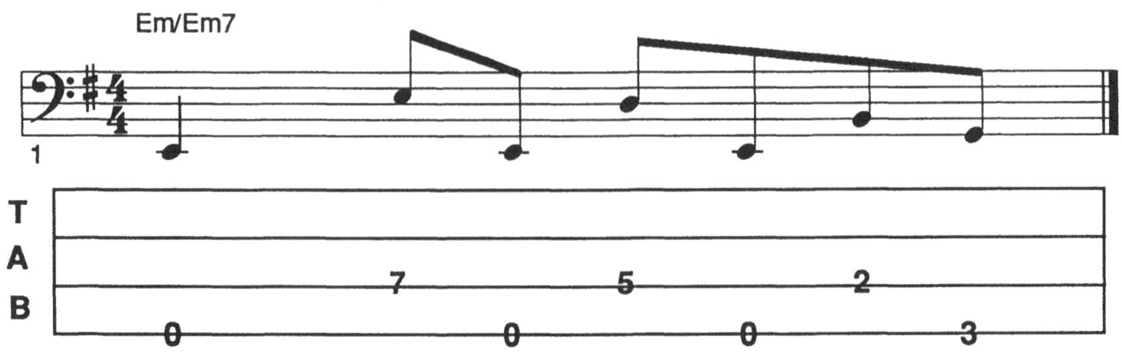

Example 19

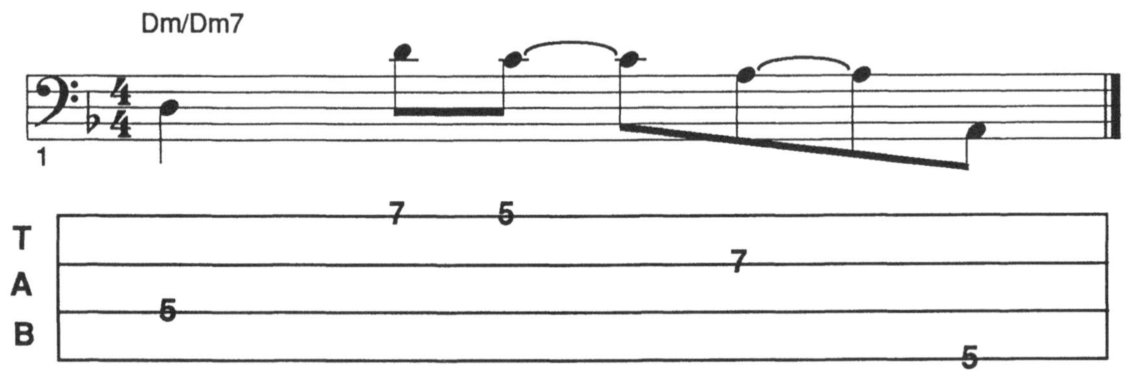

Example 20

Example 21

Example 22

Walking Bass Lines . . . .

Walking bass lines are probably the most recognizable bass lines around. Although they are mostly associated with blues and jazz, they apply to everything. So here are about 20 different variations on walking bass lines. As with the major and minor lines before, concentrate on learning the pattern and how it relates to the chord being played. That is the key to making up your own walking bass lines!! Have fun....

Example 23

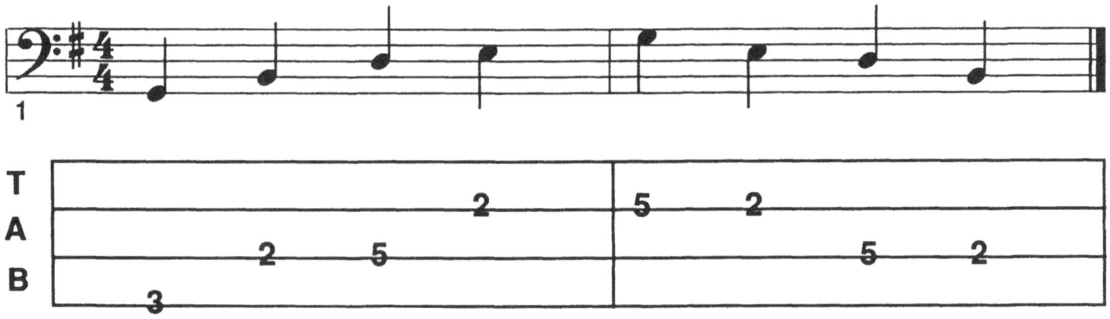

Example 24

Example 25

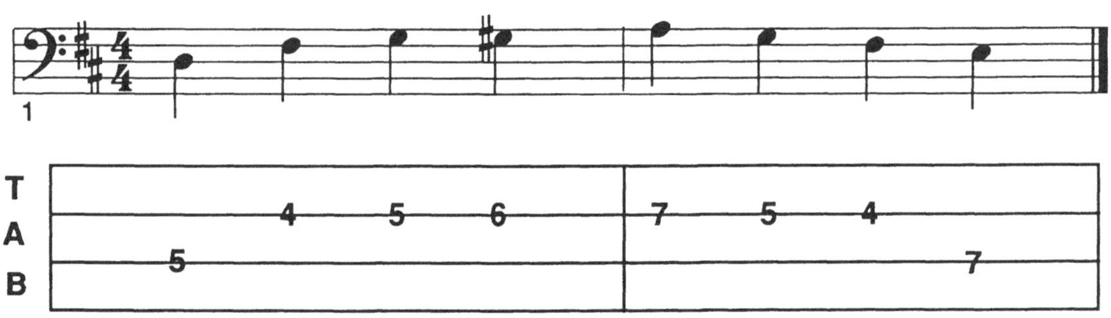

Example 26

Example 27

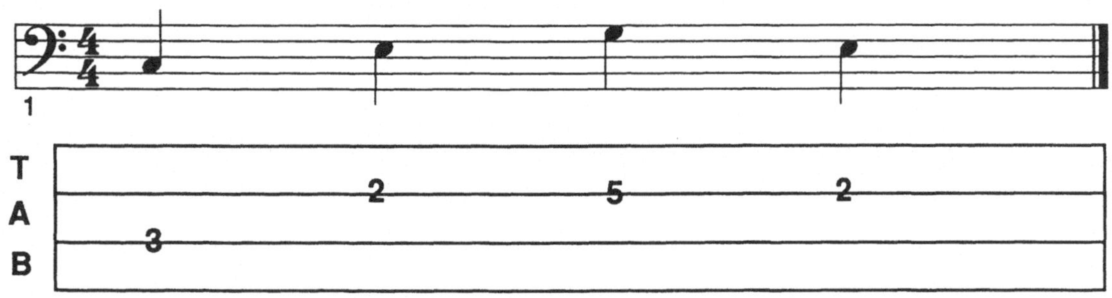

Example 28

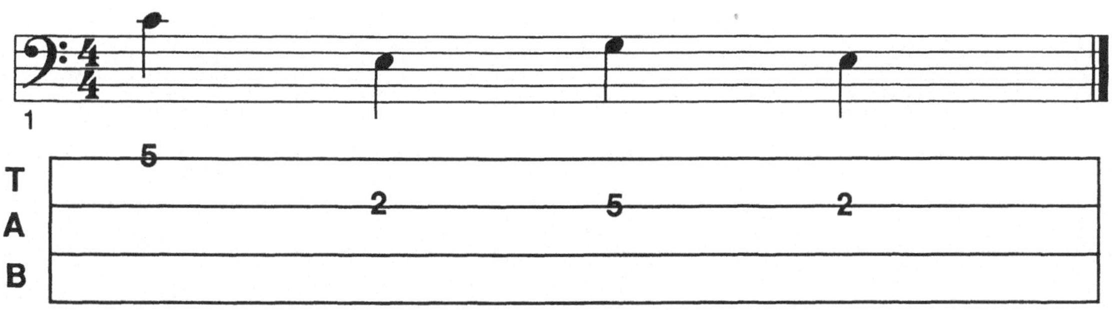

Example 29

Example 30

Example 31

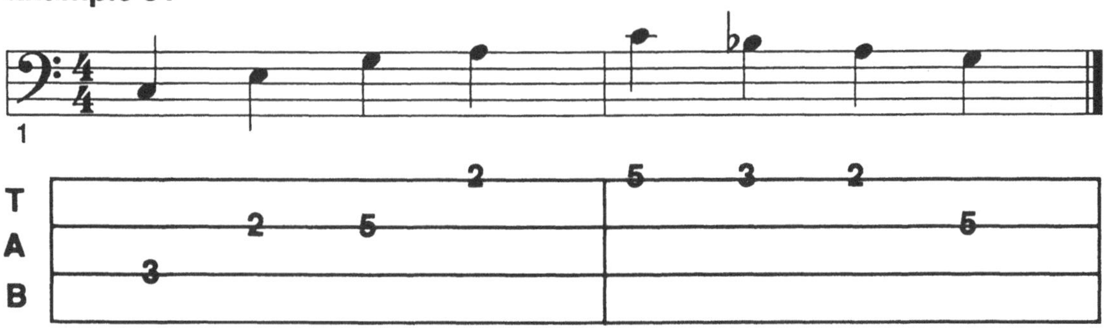

Example 32

Example 33

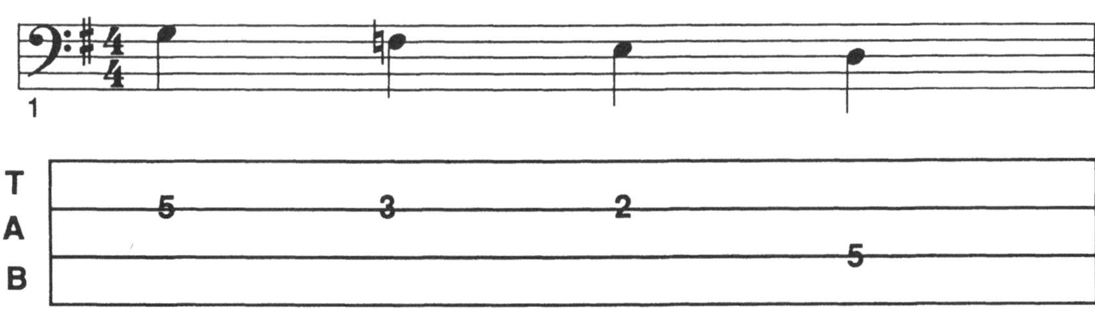

Example 34

Example 35

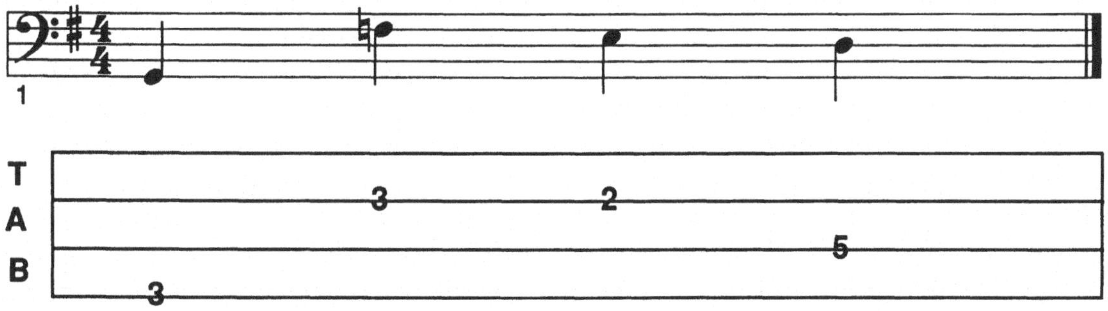

Example 36

Example 37

Example 38

Example 39

Example 40

Example 41

Example 42

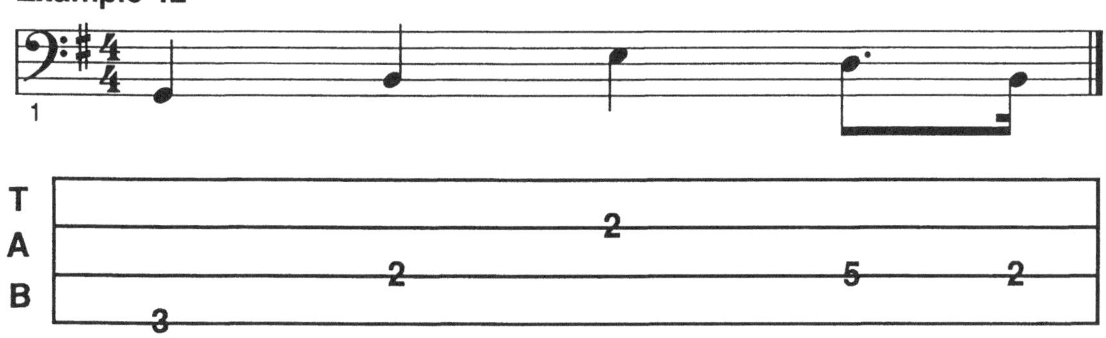

Slap-and-Pop Technique

The slap technique is one of the most popular techniques used in modern bass playing. You can hardly listen to the radio for more than two songs without hearing the bass player slap or pop something!

Slap playing is also one of the most challenging and fun techniques to master. It is a study of rhythm more than anything else. Variations on rhythm patterns are a very key element in slap.

To do this, a large "library" of different rhythm patterns is required. Also, a very solid understanding of the rhythm patterns involved helps you to create different patterns and variations on patterns you are already familiar with.

Right-Hand Technique

The right hand is the key to the slap technique, mainly because it's the hand that does the "slappin' "! The basic technique is to slap the string *against the fretboard* using the right thumb. The act of slapping must be a very quick and accurate attack on the string. A couple of important things to remember are to always keep your right hand and forearm relaxed so it's easier to move freely, and that there's really no need to do your Mr. T impersonation and break your thumb because you slap the string too hard! You can't play slap with a cast on your hand!

Hand placement is important. Your right hand must be in a position that is relaxed, comfortable, easy to move, and free to do all of the things you must do. I will describe how and where to place the right hand. You should try to do it exactly as I describe, then over time you can make adjustments that will allow you to feel the most comfortable.

Place your right hand so that the right thumb is almost parallel to the fourth string (a slight angle is okay). Position your right hand so that the right thumb is just over the last fret or so of the fretboard. At this time the right-hand fingers should be lying flat across the strings. The back "fleshy" part of your right hand (the heel) should be touching the fourth string. Let's talk about what role each of the three parts of your right hand will play when you slap:

The THUMB: **The thumb will be used to slap the strings. You will need to learn to slap all four of the strings (individually). To slap a note, quickly slap the string against the fretboard with the thumb. The thumb should "bounce" back off of the string very quickly, so as not to kill or mute the note when it is slapped.**

The HEEL: The heel will be used to mute, or deaden, selected notes. One common use will be to keep lower strings from ringing when you are playing on the first, second, and third strings. Developing control over the use of the heel of the right hand is very tricky and just as important.

The FINGERS: The first and second fingers will be used to "pop" notes on the first, second, and sometimes third strings. Popping is done by curving the fingertip under the string and pulling the string away from the fretboard, then releasing the string so that the string slaps back against the fretboard. Be very careful not to grab the string with too much of the finger, as you may pull the string right off of the bass! Use the first finger to pop notes on the second and third strings, and use the second finger to pop notes on the first string.

The act of slapping and popping should be a "down-up" technique. Follow me as I explain what I mean by "down-up":

1. In order to slap or pop any note, the hand must first be raised away from the strings.

2. To slap a note, the entire right hand is brought down to allow the thumb to slap the note against the fretboard as described above. This is the *down* stroke.

3. Once again, to slap or pop another note, the hand must be raised away from the strings. As the hand is being raised, popped notes are played with the first or second finger. This is the *up* stroke. If the next note is supposed to be slapped instead of popped, you would raise the hand and then slap the second note.

Popped notes are played on the up stroke *after* a slapped note.

Left-Hand Technique

The left hand provides the "finesse" in slap playing. With the left hand you will hold, choke, add vibrato, bend, trill, slide, hammer, (and on and on...) the notes that your right hand is dishing out. If you are playing open strings, the left hand is used to cut off, or "choke," the notes to provide a more staccato feel.

In the exercises to follow, you should try each experiment using different feels with the left hand. Try 'em with vibrato or without vibrato. Cut the notes short, or let them ring long. Try different approaches to establish your own library of techniques and feels with the left hand. In the exercises that follow, I will make suggestions on left-hand exercises and techniques, as well.

Okay, let's play some. We'll start out simply to establish the proper technique. Then we will learn some different rhythm patterns. After that, we will learn how to create variations on given rhythm patterns. Have a good time with this stuff — it's really fun!!

Slap Exercises

As I mentioned before, slap playing is a serious study in rhythm. In the exercises that follow, we will be experimenting with different variations on quarter and eighth notes. Repeat the rhythm pattern until you feel as though you are in the groove of the pattern.

I strongly recommend that you practice with a metronome or a drum machine when doing these exercises. This will really help you develop a good sense of timing and rhythm. You can even program the drum machine to play the exact same rhythm pattern you are working on. Then you have a steady reference of what the pattern should sound like.

One more piece of advice, then I'll shut up and let you play.... **GO SLOWLY!!!** Slow down and you'll go faster! It is very important to go slowly and make sure you get the basics of the technique down cold. If your foundation is weak, your playing will have poor timing, control, and feel. Speed comes with time. Allow yourself that time, and you'll be much better off.

To start out, play the following quarter-note rhythm patterns using the slap method described above. These exercises use only the right-hand thumb; there is no popping yet. Play them slowly until you develop a rhythm and a consistent feel from one pattern to the next. Each note should be strong, solid, and well defined. Use the left hand to let the notes ring as true quarter notes, the full length of the beat.

Note that this exercise is written with *all notes being the open E-string.* After you feel comfortable with the rhythm patterns, try the same rhythms using the G and then the A notes on the 3rd and 5th frets of the E-string to get used to the left-hand technique when slapping.

Slap 1

Okay, here comes the eighth-note study. Do this one the same way as the quarter-note study above, except this time use the left hand to let the notes ring long and to cut off or choke the notes for a more staccato feel. So, first learn the rhythm patterns letting the notes ring for their full values. Then go back and try to change to a more staccato feel by choking the notes with the left hand. (Choking is done by lifting the left hand off of the fretboard without letting the string ring freely. It is advisable to allow all four fingers on the left hand to touch the string to stop it from vibrating, thus choking it.)

This exercise is written in the open A-string. Try it using the G (E-string), C (A-string), and any other notes on either the A- or E-strings.

Here comes an exercise that mixes quarter-note and eighth-note patterns, sometimes even in the same bar, so I hope you did your homework! Get this exercise down good and solid, because next we're gonna start poppin'!!

Slap 3

Pop Exercises

As mentioned before, popping is done using the right-hand first finger to pop the second string, and the right-hand second finger to pop the first string. Let's get used to the idea and feel of popping notes before we start combining slapping and popping. This is where the left-hand technique really comes into play. A popped note does not sustain very long. And if you let it ring, it's usually not a very attractive sound. So, most of the time you must choke or cut off the note, making it pretty short. The more you pop notes, the better you will get at working the left hand to really get the most tone out of the note.

For the following exercises, you need to concentrate on getting a good, solid, and clear tone out of each note. Also, you need to get the first and second fingers on your right hand used to the feel of popping so they always grab just enough of the string to get a good pop without getting your hand "caught up" under the string.

So, here's an exercise that is ALL POPPING. Do not slap any of these notes. Remember to pop the notes on the G-string with the second finger, and the notes on the D-string with the first finger. Check the tablature below to see where to play each note.

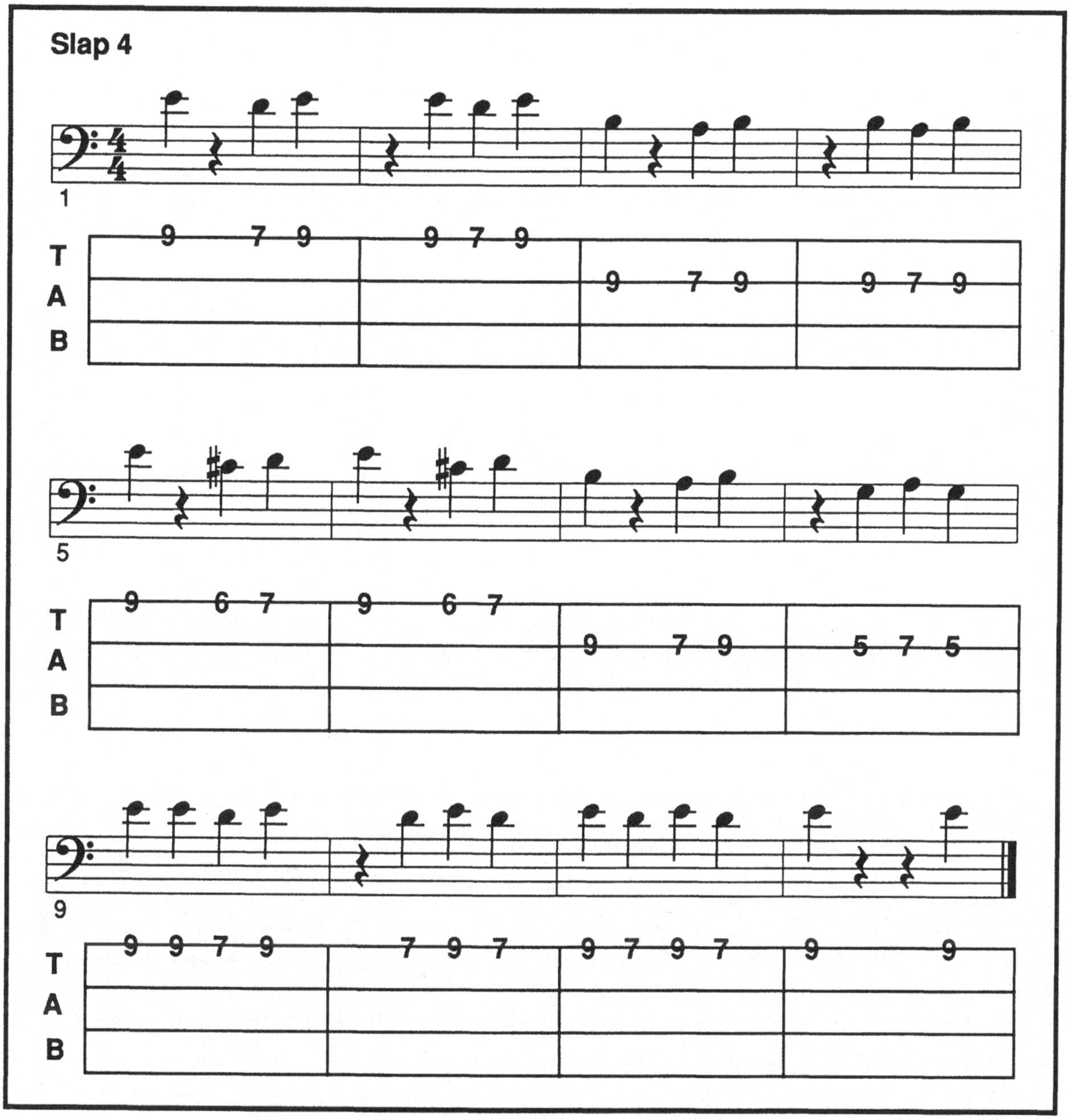

Okay, now let's try alternating slaps and pops. Without a doubt, the most common pattern for the slap technique is the octave pattern (remember disco??). It is done simply by alternating between a note and the next higher octave of that same note.

The pattern below is an example of a quarter-note octave pattern. Remember, when you are alternating slapping and popping, you should use the down-up technique I described earlier. That is, the slap is the down stroke; then, when you are bringing your right hand back up, you do the pop (the up stroke). The goal is a smooth, easy rhythm of down-up-down-up.... Try it on the quarter-note pattern.

Slap 5

Now, here is an eighth-note octave pattern to work with. Use both this eighth-note pattern and the above quarter-note pattern to really get familiar with the feeling of slapping and popping.

Slap 6

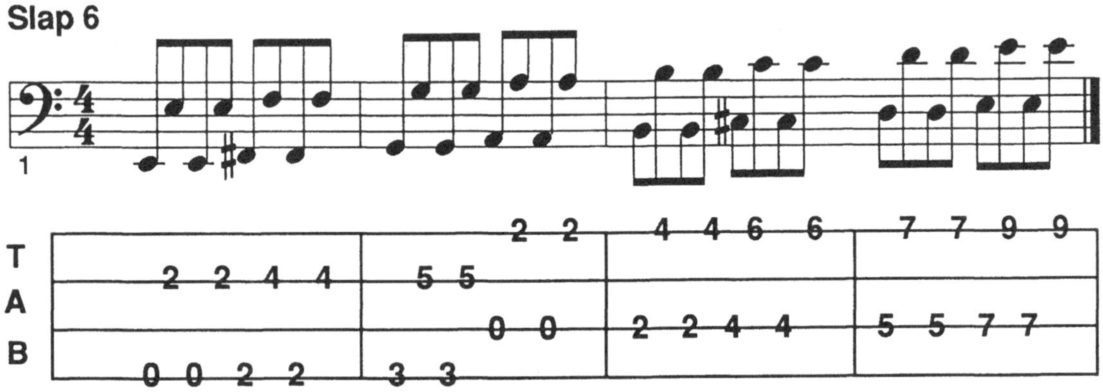

Technique Exercises

Here is an octave-pattern technique exercise to really get you used to slapping and popping. Use this as a warm-up exercise before you start playing. Play it *slowly* at first, then build up some speed.

Simple Rhythm Patterns . . . .

Here are a few simple rhythm patterns to get you used to playing some different combinations of slap/pop alternations. Use the tablature to see where to play the notes. Again, experiment with different left-hand techniques to allow the notes to sustain or be choked.

Slap 8

Slap 9

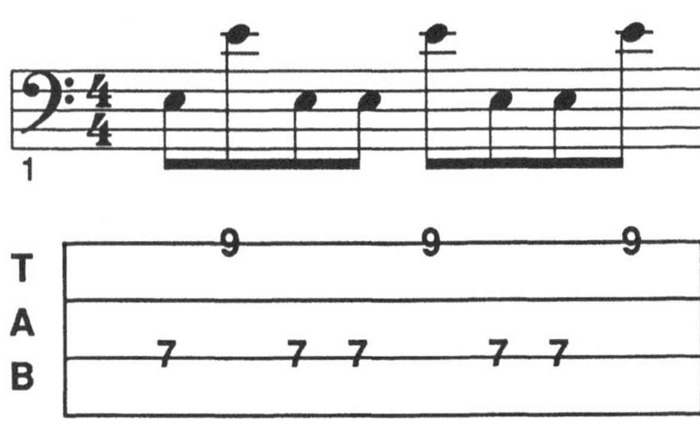

Slap 10

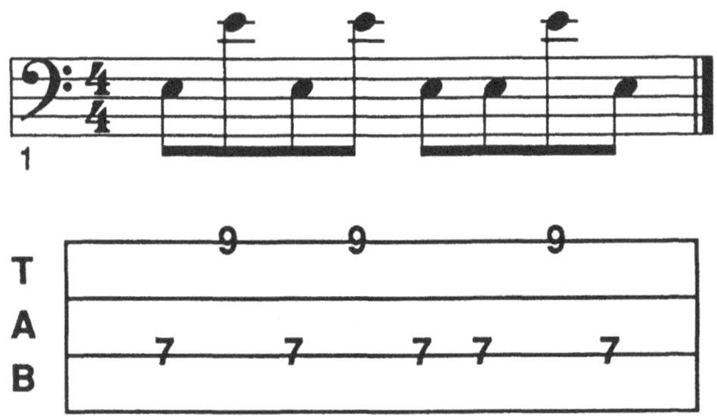

Slap 11

More Rhythm Patterns

Here are a few rhythm patterns to work with. I'm throwing in some eighth- and sixteenth-note combinations to give you some other ideas. Notice the letters above the musical exercises. Now that we're going to be mixing up different notes and rhythm patterns, I will start identifying which notes are slapped with the right thumb (T = thumb) and popped (P = popped).

Slap 12

Slap 13

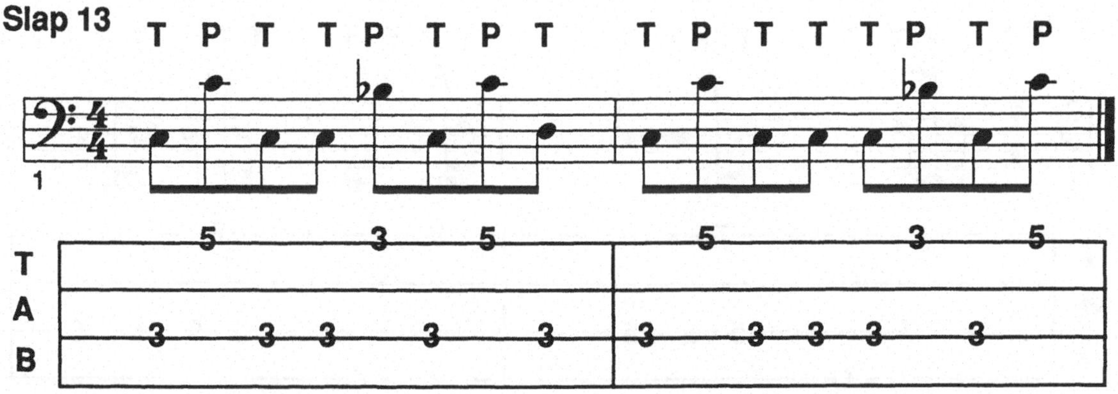

Slap 14

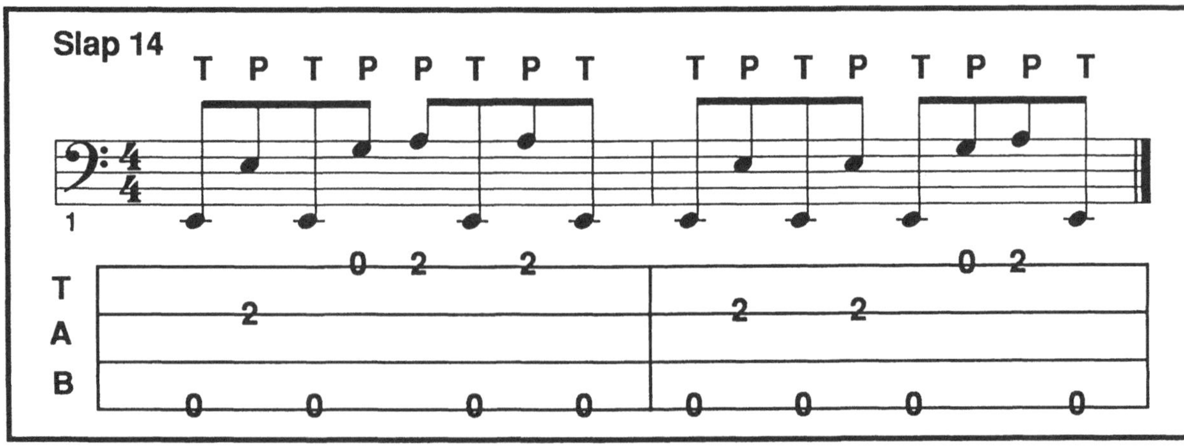

Slap 15

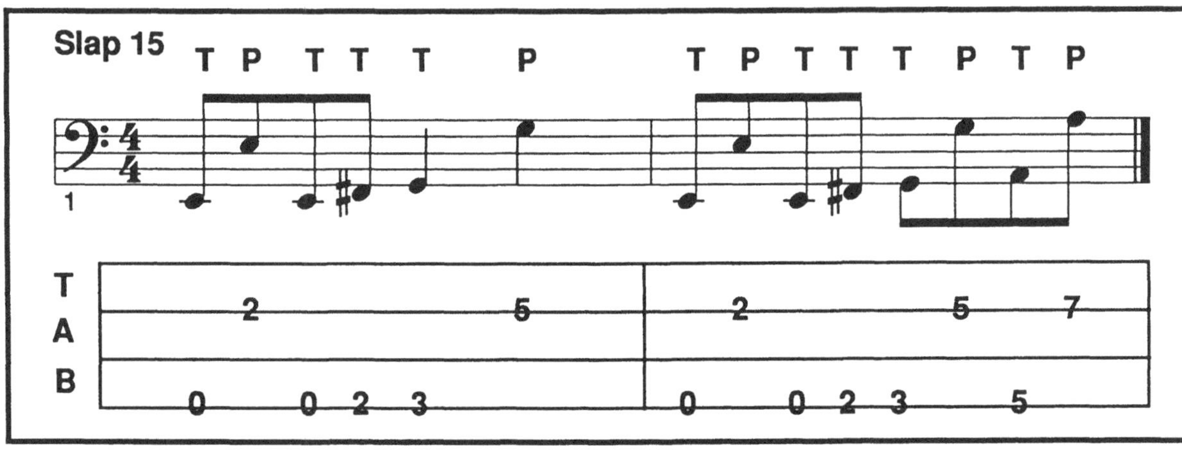

Slap 16

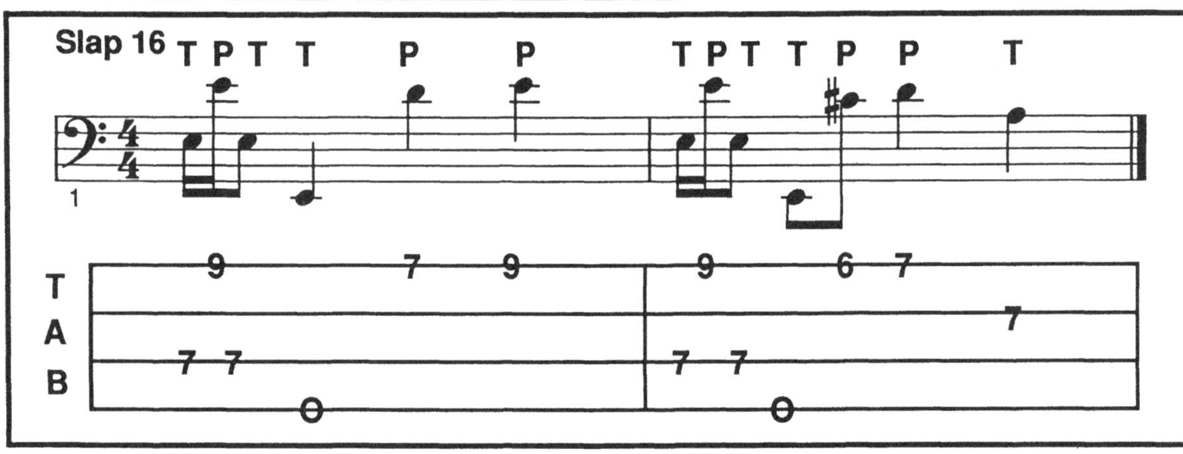

Slap 17

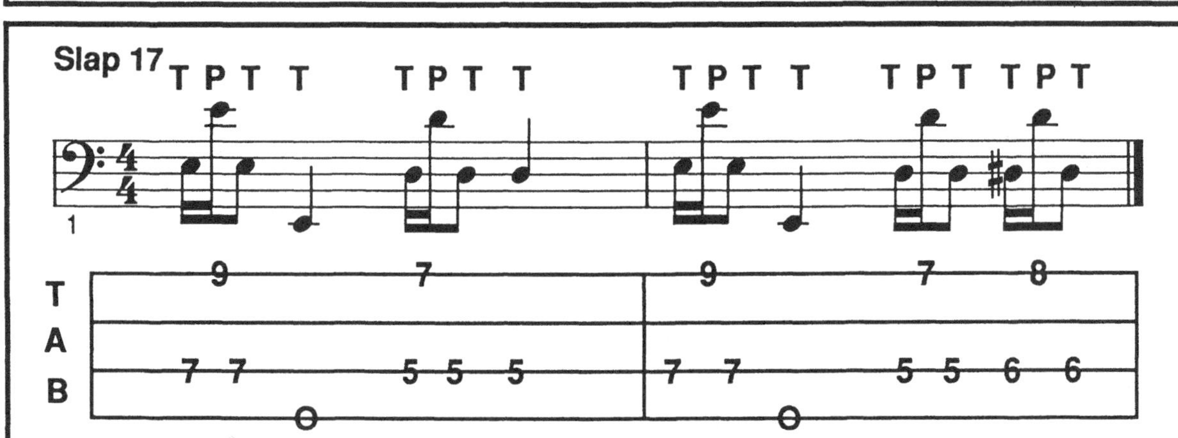

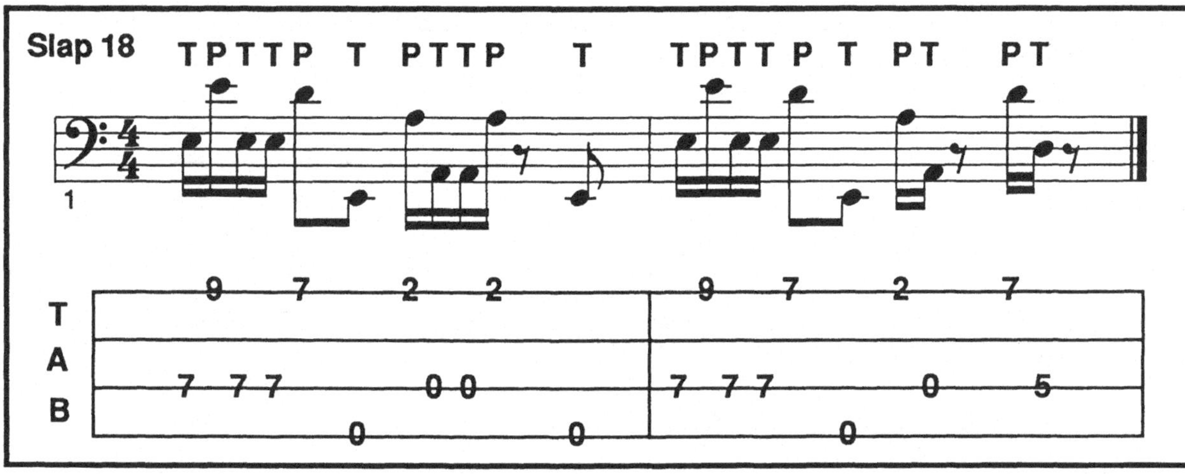

Hammer-Ons and Pull-Offs

Sounds like a game show, doesn't it? Actually, hammer-ons and pull-offs are the most important part of the slap-and-pop technique, with the exception of the actual slapping and popping!

Hammer-ons and pull-offs are techniques that are used by the left hand to create different effects. In slap-and-pop playing, while the left hand is hammering-on and pulling-off, the right hand may be slapping or popping; it works both ways. Let's take a look at hammer-ons and pull-offs....

A hammer-on usually consists of two notes, sometimes more than two (but never less than two). The first note is picked (or slapped or popped). The second note is sounded by fretting it with a left-hand finger, but without picking it again. Some extra force may be required to sound out the second note. The effect is a sort of "slurring" effect because the second note is not picked. Hammer-ons are between two notes on the same string, within one to five frets' distance of each other (or however far your hand can stretch).

In the exercise below, you will be slapping on each beat and hammering to the eighth note between the beats.

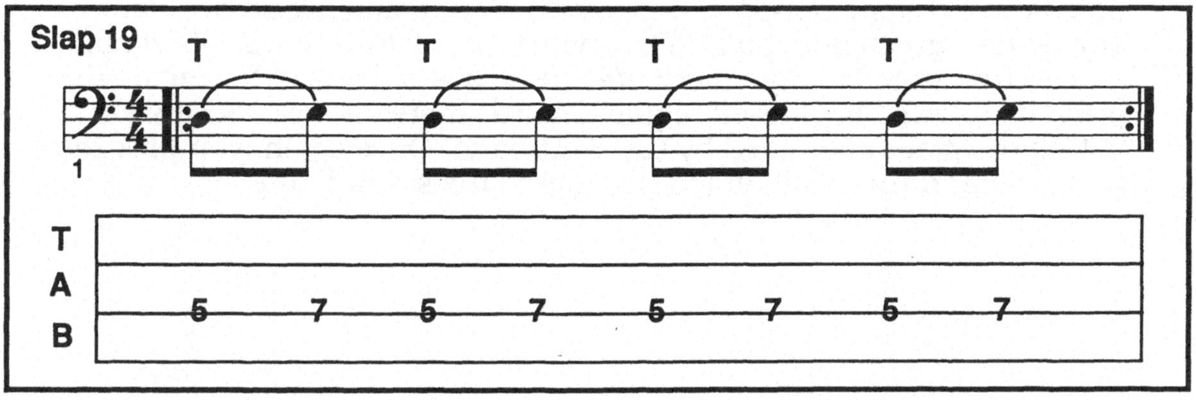

In this exercise, you will be popping on each beat and hammering to the eighth note between the beats.

Slap 20

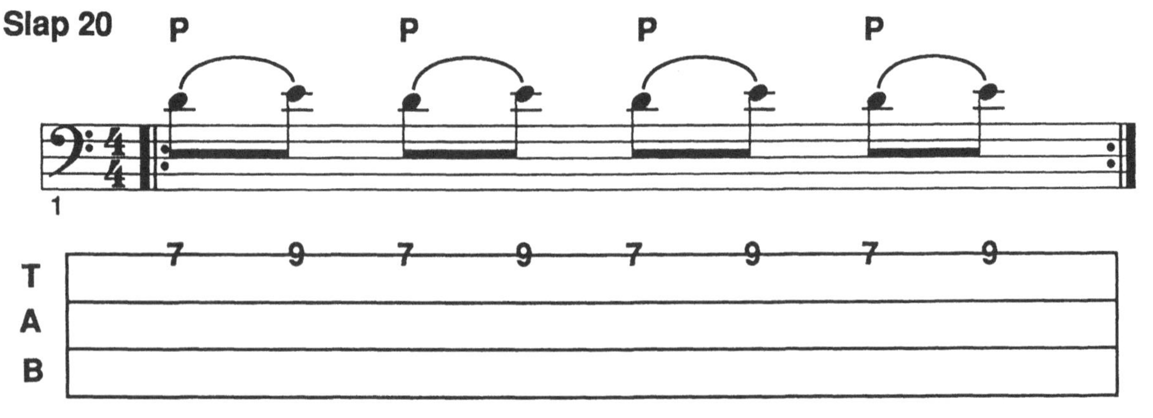

Practice alternating slapping and popping hammer-ons like this:

Slap 21

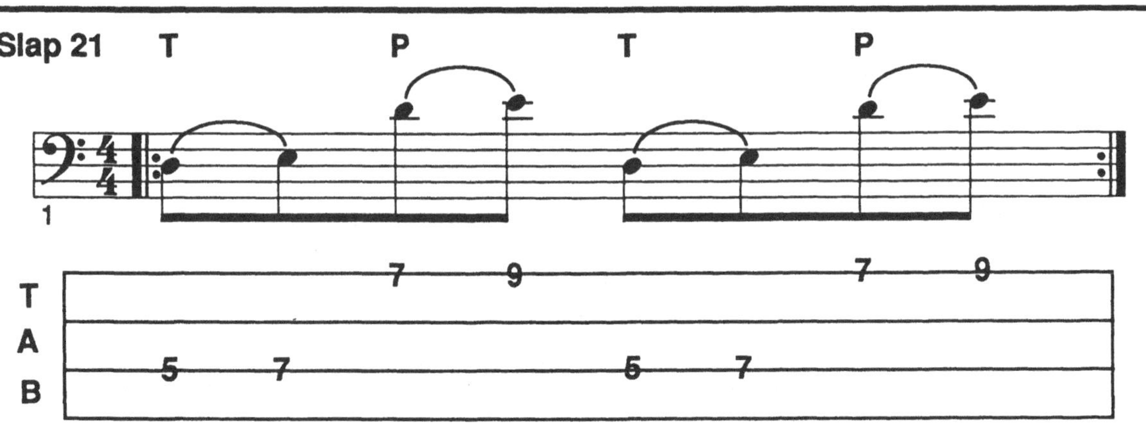

A pull-off is almost the exact opposite of a hammer-on. The first note is picked (or slapped or popped...); then, using a kind of sideways and downward motion, pull-off to a note that is lower than the first note. Be careful not to let any other notes be struck or caused to ring by the pull-off motion. The pull-off requires a little more strength because it is taking the place of a "pick" by the right hand. Once again, you pick the first note and then pull-off (no picking) to the second note.

The following exercise should be slapped. (And we know how painful that can be!) Sorry. Slap each of the notes that fall on the beat, and pull-off to the eighth notes between the beats.

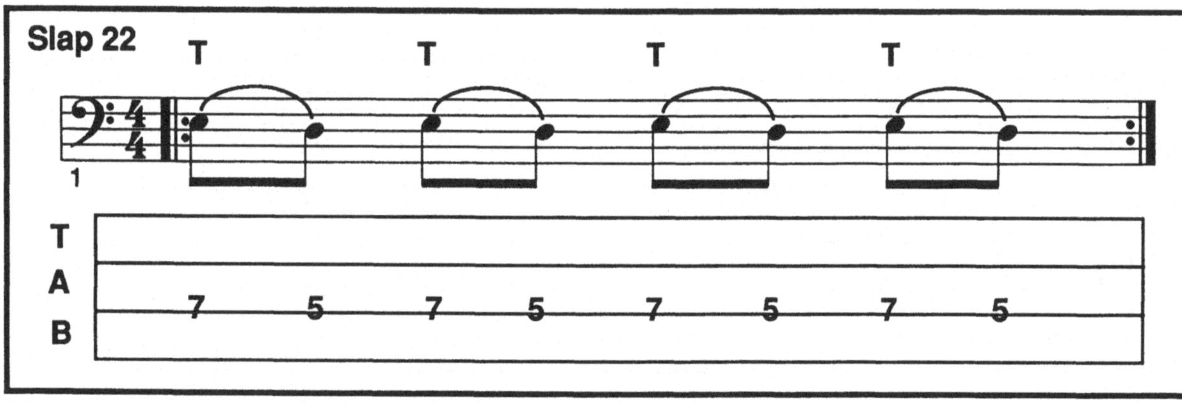

The following exercise should be popped. Pop each of the notes that falls on the beat, and pull-off to the eighth notes between the beats.

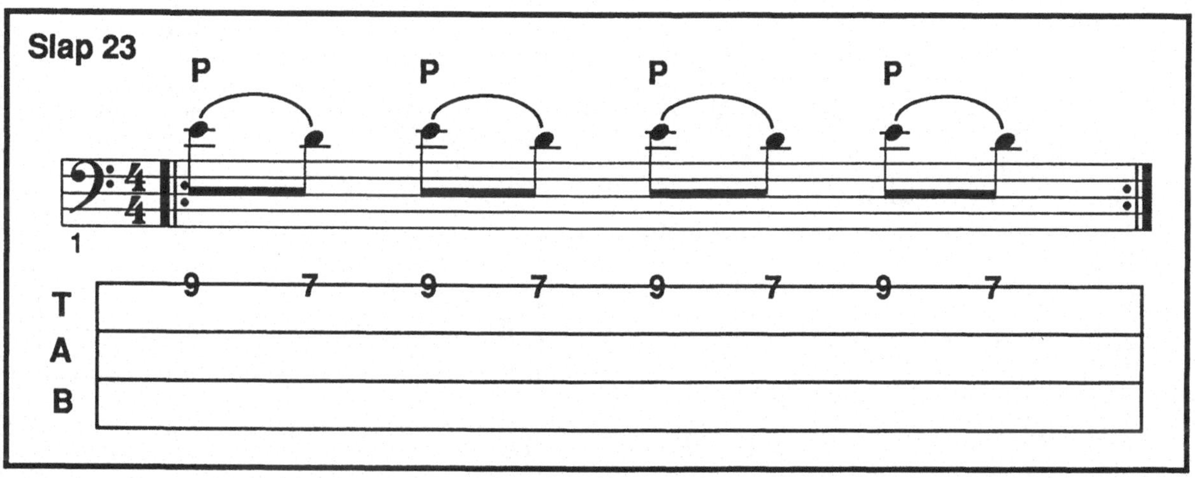

Here's one that alternates slapping and popping using pull-offs:

Slap 24

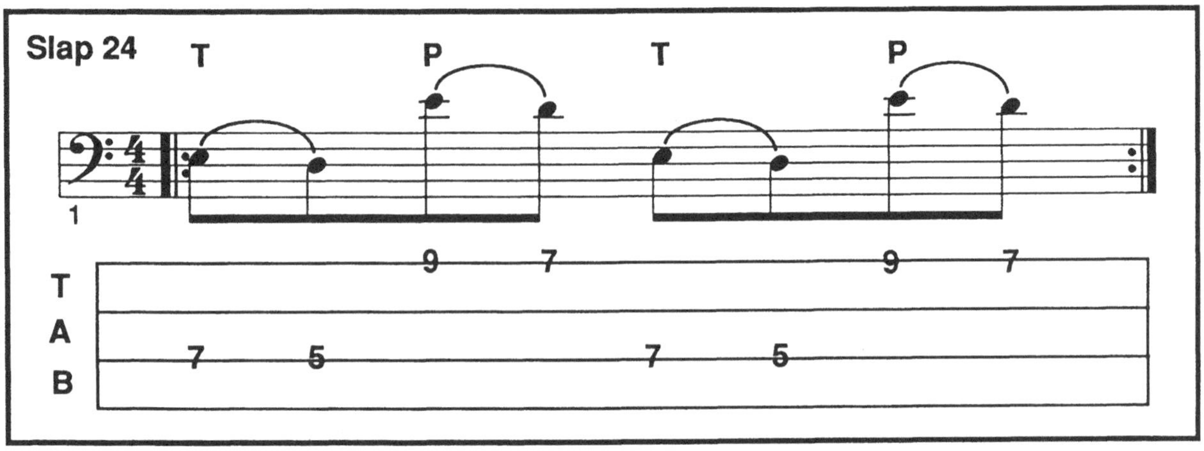

Okay, let's try alternating hammer-ons and pull-offs while slapping and popping, all wrapped up into one exercise:

Slap 25

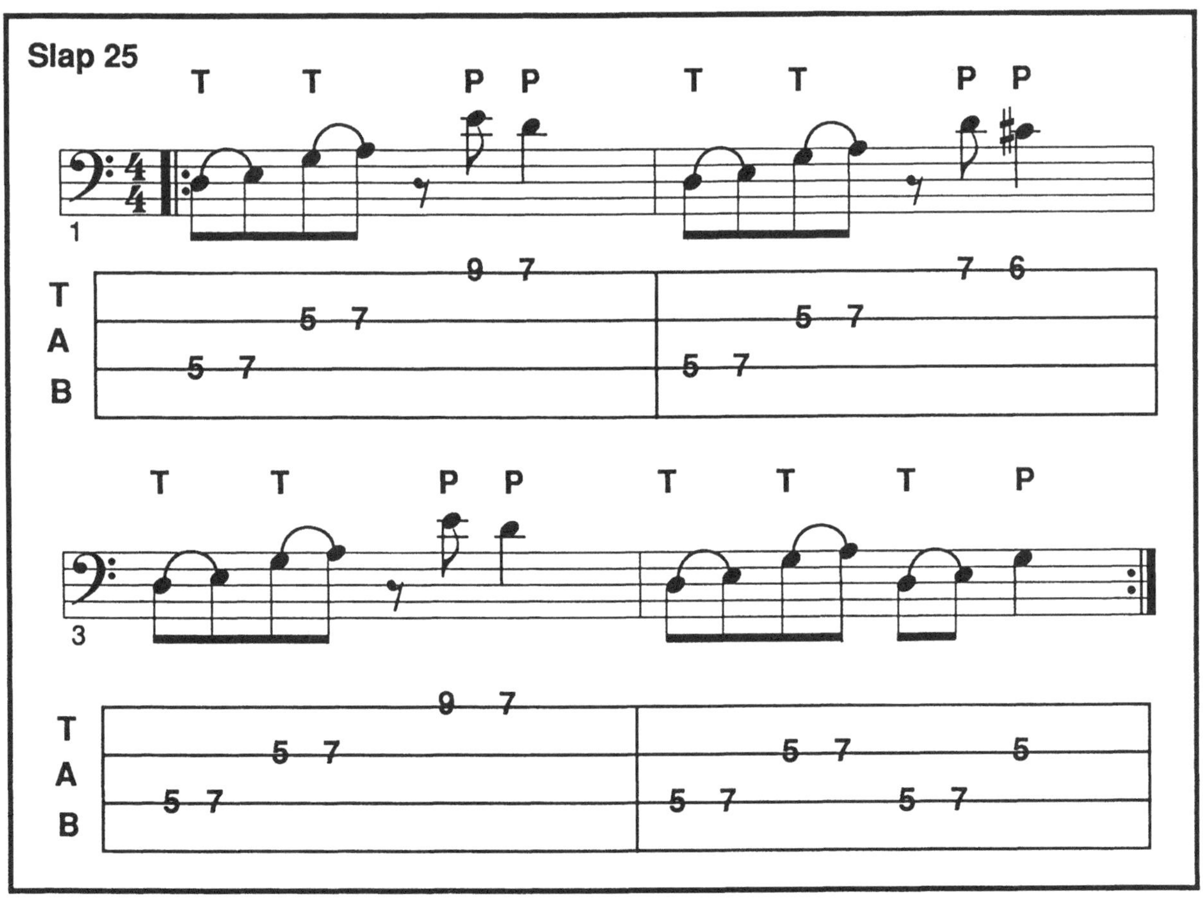

Here are a couple of lines using slapped and popped hammer-ons and pull-offs:

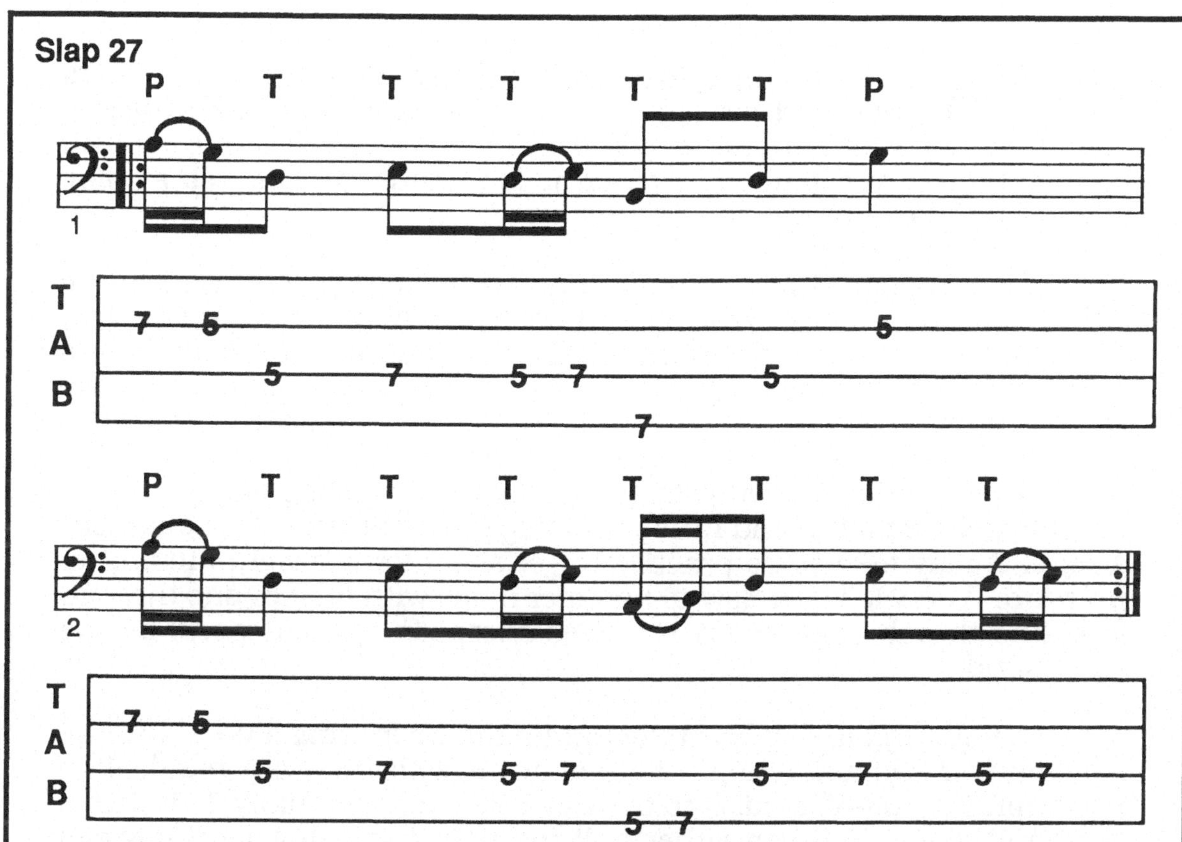

Well, that should help get you started on your way to "Slapdom"!! There are many books available that can help you expand your slap capabilities. Look into it and have a good time!!

Right-Hand Hammering Technique

Since it was first popularized by rock guitar players in the late '70s, right-hand hammering has become a very important part of rock guitar playing. It has also become a very important part of contemporary rock bass playing.

While the technique is sometimes viewed as a "flashy" or "showy" technique that should be used merely as a show-stopper or attention grabber, it can also be used as a serious part of any bass player's repertoire of techniques. Listen to how players like Stuart Hamm and Billy Sheehan have used this technique in a very musical sense, without abandoning the context of the songs they are playing. It is a very useful technique to have available, should you need it.

I will demonstrate the technique for use in both the "flash" and song contexts. First, we will learn the basic technique and concept for playing right-hand hammer-ons using four fingers of the right hand.

Right-Hand Technique

The right hand is going to be used to do hammer-ons and pull-offs of notes on the fretboard either above or below the left hand. By doing this in conjunction with hammer-ons and pull-offs by the left hand, you will be able to play sweeping lines covering large intervals, as well as play those very quick lines.

To hammer-on and pull-off notes with the right hand, slide the right hand up the neck to the area where it is to play. When you do this, the right thumb should slide right up the top edge of the neck and act as a counterbalancing force against the hammering and pulling-off by the right-hand fingers.

A note is *hammered* with the right hand by bringing your right-hand finger over a fret and firmly pressing down the string to sound out a note. It may take some practice to get a feel for the right amount of pressure. You will learn how to hammer notes with fingers one through four (the thumb is generally not used except in special cases) on the right hand.

A note is *pulled-off* with the right hand by fretting a note with the left hand, then hammering a note above it with the right hand, then performing a pull-off similar to the way you would normally do it with a left-hand finger. You can either pull the right-hand finger up towards your body or push it down towards the ground to do the pull-off. I prefer to pull up towards the body. You should experiment with both to determine which way feels best and allows you the most control over your right hand.

A note can also be pulled-off from one right-hand finger to another right-hand finger. This takes a great deal of control and strength in each of the right-hand fingers. We will play some exercises to help develop the necessary strength.

Left-Hand Technique . . . .

One might think, in a chapter called "Right-Hand Hammering Technique," that the left hand has little to do. Oh, how wrong one would be!! The fact is, the right hand is simply imitating a technique that we have been doing with the left hand for quite some time: hammer-ons and pull-offs. We do it in straight bass-playing techniques, and we do it in slap techniques. Now we're just going to expand it to include the right hand.

So the basic job of the left hand is simply to hammer-on and pull-off notes in conjunction with the right hand. So be sure that your hammer-on and pull-off skills are pretty good. They will only get better when you incorporate the right-hand hammering technique into your "toolbox." You should be prepared to hammer-on and pull-off notes on the same string, as well as those that lie on different strings (i.e. octaves, 3rds, typical double stops...).

It is very important to develop the technique so that there is no volume or tone difference between notes played with the right hand and the left hand. They should all sound the same. With practice, you will find this to be fairly simple. Don't be afraid to get into this and just "manhandle" these bass lines. This can be a pretty aggressive technique, so don't hesitate to reach down and grab these notes! Make 'em count!! Let's play somethin'....

Right-Hand Hammering . . . .

The first thing we'll do is learn how to play a series of hammer-ons and pull-offs using both the right and left hands. Use this opportunity to develop some coordination between the two hands.

In the following exercise, the B note is played on the D-string with the first finger of the right hand. The A note is played on the D-string with the fourth finger of the left hand. To begin, play the A as you would a normal note by picking it with your right hand. Then reach up with the right hand and hammer-on the B using the first finger of the right hand. Make sure it is a good, solid-sounding note, similar in tone to the A that was played before it. That is how you hammer-on a note with the right hand.

The left hand should still be holding down the A with the fourth finger. Next, while still holding down the B (it should still be ringing), pull-off the B with the first finger of the right hand to the A (fourth finger of the left hand). Make sure that the pull-off is clean and smooth sounding. For reference, try hammering-on the A and B using only the left hand. The right-hand hammering method should sound the same. Here's what it looks like:

NOTE: The "L4" stands for left hand, fourth finger; and the "R1" stands for the right hand, first finger. ("L3" is L.H., third finger, etc....)

Exercise 1

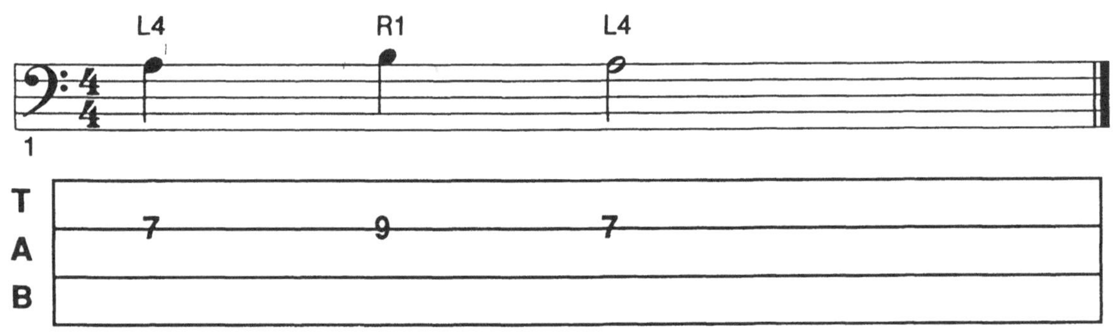

Now try repeating that type of pattern over and over. You should pick only one note, and that is the first one (A). The rest of the notes are to be played by hammering-on and pulling-off with the right hand (first finger). Again, make sure that both your rhythm and tone are consistent from note to note.

Exercise 2

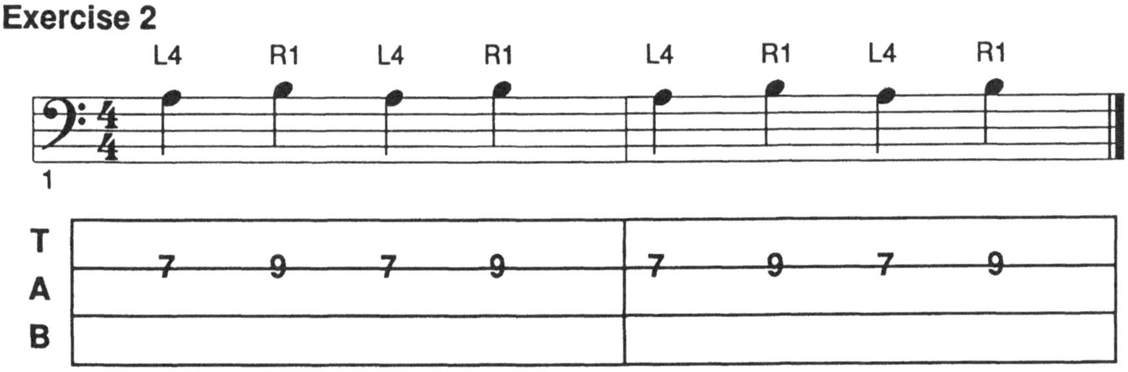

Before we start talking about using all four fingers of the right hand to hammer-on and pull-off, let's concentrate on the first finger of the right hand and getting used to this whole method of playing.

Probably the most common use of the right-hand hammering technique is to play a repeating pattern of either 3 eighth-note triplets or 4 sixteenth notes. Let's take a look at those two ideas.

The 3-eighth-note triplet idea involves two notes that are played by the left hand and one note played by the right hand. You can start the pattern with either the left or right hand. Let's start with the left hand first. The three notes we will use are G, A, and B on the D-string (5th, 7th, and 9th frets).

First, pick the G with the right hand, then hammer-on the A using the fourth finger of the left hand. Next, hammer-on the B using the first finger of the right hand. Those are the first three notes of the exercise written below. To continue the pattern, pull-off the B with the right hand to the G. The G is the first note of the second set of triplets. The notes are G–A–B–G–A–B–G–A–B–G....

Try the following exercise slowly and, as you feel more comfortable, develop some speed.

Exercise 3

Now let's try starting with the right hand. The first note is the B played with the first finger of the right hand. Pull-off to the A (fourth finger, left hand), then pull-off to the G (first finger, left hand). Repeat the pattern as B-A-G-B-A-G-B-A-G.... Here's what it looks like:

Exercise 4

There is another way to play the pattern starting with the right hand. That is to play the B with the right hand, pull-off to the G (first finger, left hand), and then hammer-on to the A with the fourth finger of the left hand. Repeat the pattern as B-G-A-B-G-A-B-G.... Here's what it looks like:

Exercise 5

Practice each of these eighth-note triplet patterns until you have them down. Make sure you have them down well because here comes an exercise that uses all three of those combinations plus a couple of minor variations on them. This should be a fun exercise, but go slowly at first and be sure you are playing the right notes in the right order, as this exercise tends to go back and forth between notes. Play the D and E notes on the A-string. And notice that some of the G notes are also played on the A-string as well as the D-string.

Exercise 6

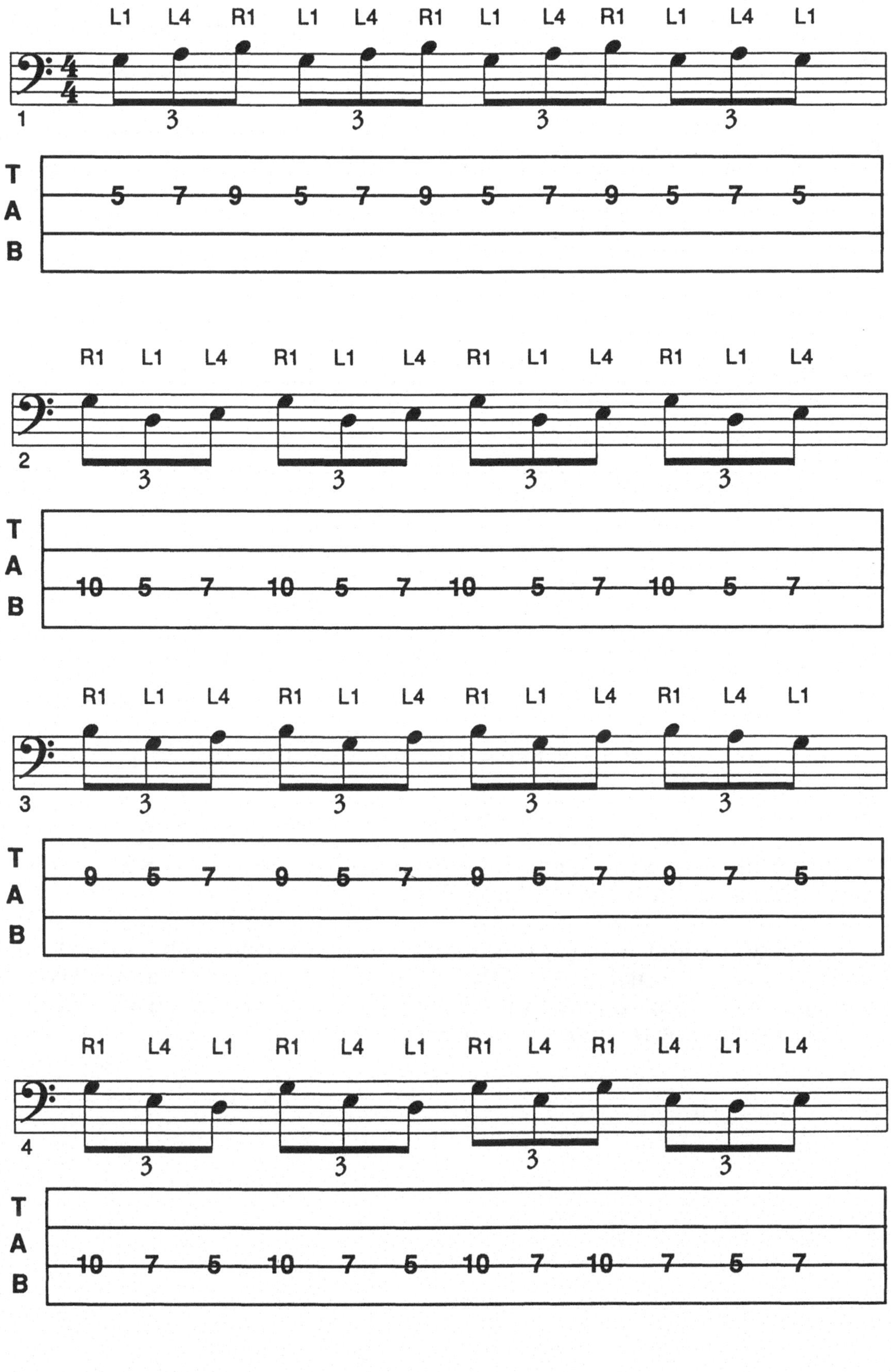
L1 L4 R1 L1 L4 R1 L1 L4 R1 L1 L4 L1
1
3 3 3 3
T A B
5 7 9 5 7 9 5 7 9 5 7 5
R1 L1 L4 R1 L1 L4 R1 L1 L4 R1 L1 L4
2
3 3 3 3
T A B
10 5 7 10 5 7 10 5 7 10 5 7
R1 L1 L4 R1 L1 L4 R1 L1 L4 R1 L4 L1
3
3 3 3 3
T A B
9 5 7 9 5 7 9 5 7 9 7 5
R1 L4 L1 R1 L4 L1 R1 L4 R1 L4 L1 L4
4
3 3 3 3
T A B
10 7 5 10 7 5 10 7 10 7 5 7

Okay, now let's try some of those 4-sixteenth-note patterns I mentioned before....

As with the eighth-note triplet patterns, the sixteenth-note patterns can be started with either the left hand or the right hand. Let's do some that start with the left hand first.

Play the first note (G) by picking it with the right hand. Hammer-on the A with the fourth finger of the left hand, then hammer-on the B with the right hand (first finger). Pull-off the B back to the A. Those are all four notes of the pattern. Here's how it looks in print:

Exercise 7

The other way to start the pattern with the left hand is to play the A first, pull-off to the G (all left hand), then hammer-on the B with the right hand, and pull-off to the G. The G and A are left hand, and the B is the right hand. Here's how it looks:

Exercise 8

To start with the right hand, hammer-on the B with the right hand, pull-off to the A (left hand), pull-off to the G, then hammer-on the A again with the left hand. That's B–A–G–A–B–A–G–A.... Here's what it looks like:

Exercise 9

Another way to start with the right hand is to hammer-on the B, pull-off to the G, hammer-on the A, then pull-off to the G again. That looks like this:

Exercise 10

Man, I hope you did your homework on those sixteenth-note patterns because here comes an exercise that will make you work if you didn't! It uses only patterns that start with the right hand. Have fun....

Exercise 11

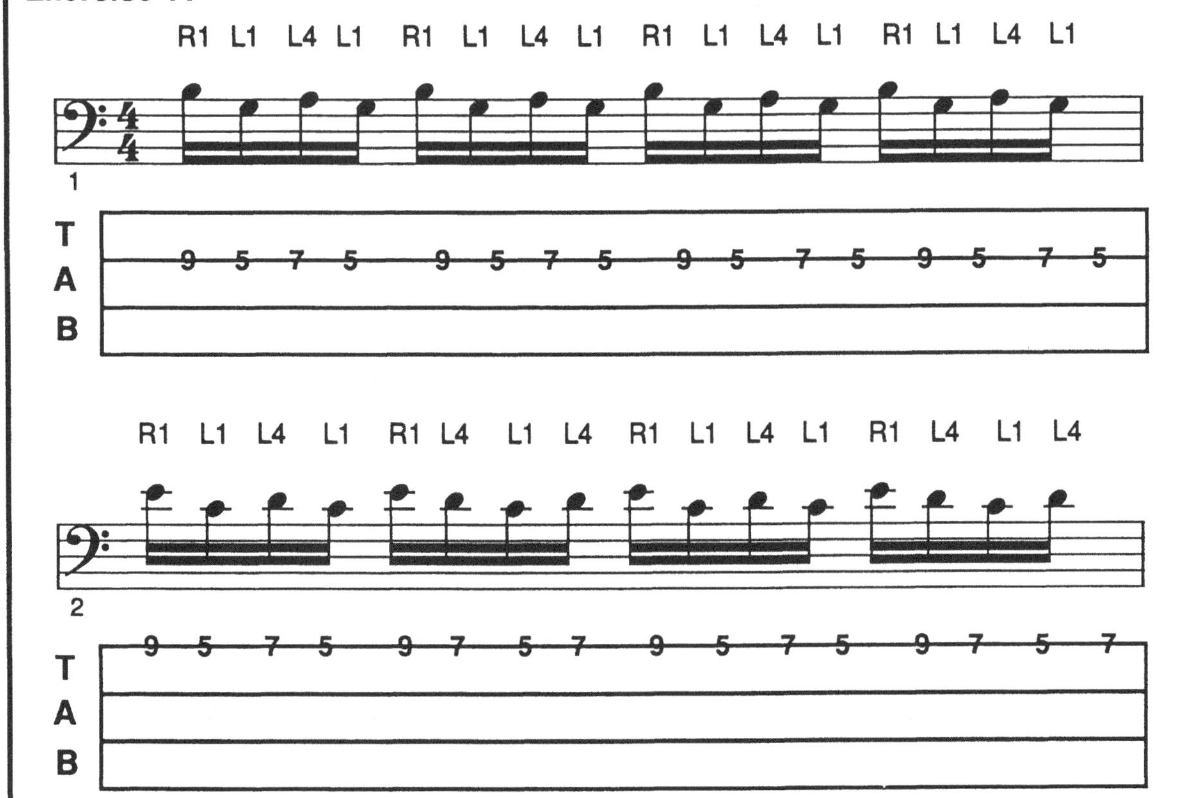

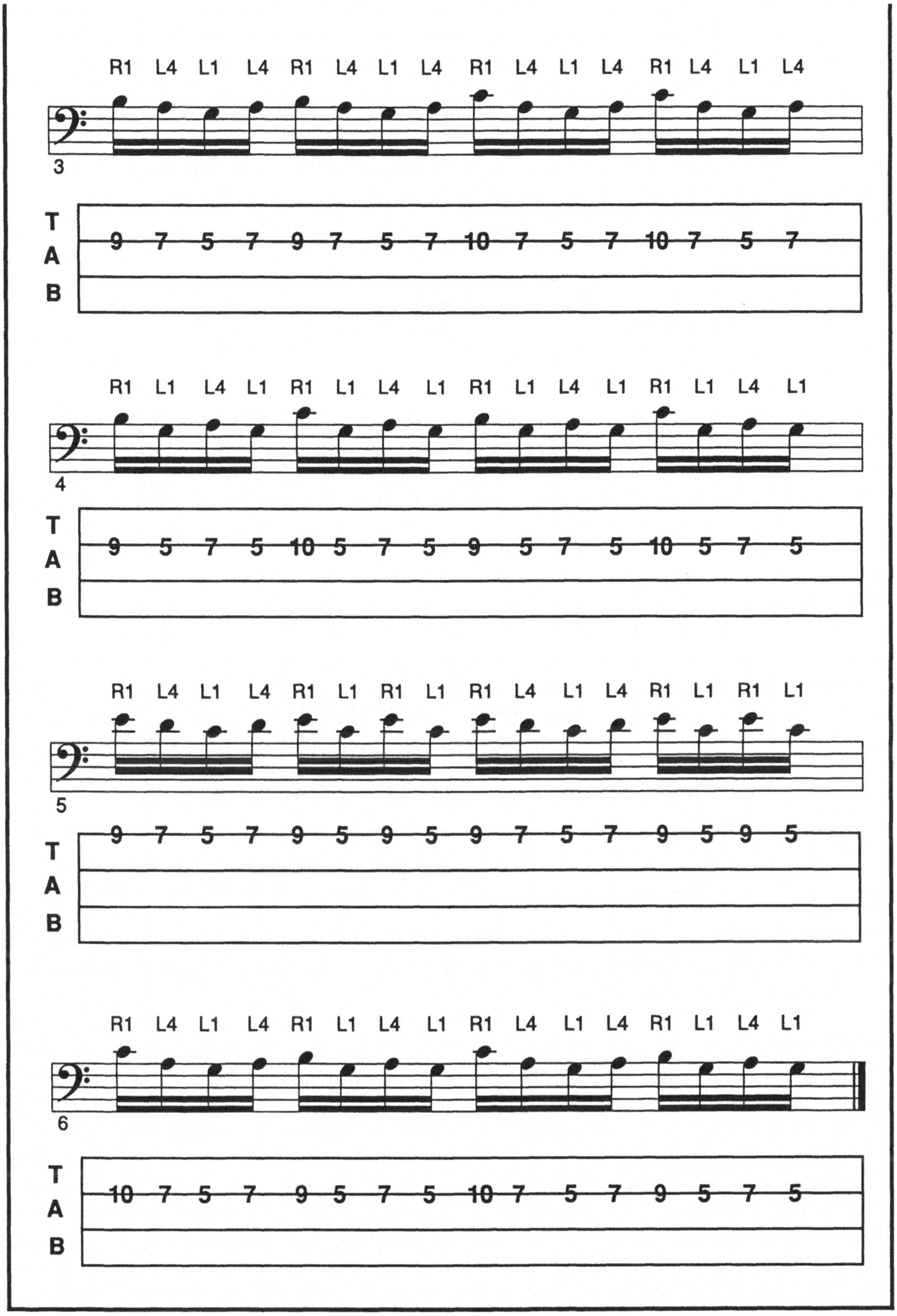
R1 L4 L1 L4 R1 L4 L1 L4 R1 L4 L1 L4 R1 L4 L1 L4
3
T A B
9 7 5 7 9 7 5 7 10 7 5 7 10 7 5 7
R1 L1 L4 L1 R1 L1 L4 L1 R1 L1 L4 L1 R1 L1 L4 L1
4
T A B
9 5 7 5 10 5 7 5 9 5 7 5 10 5 7 5
R1 L4 L1 L4 R1 L1 R1 L1 R1 L4 L1 L4 R1 L1 R1 L1
5
9 7 5 7 9 5 9 5 9 7 5 7 9 5 9 5
T A B
R1 L4 L1 L4 R1 L1 L4 L1 R1 L4 L1 L4 R1 L1 L4 L1
6
T A B
10 7 5 7 9 5 7 5 10 7 5 7 9 5 7 5

Don't be afraid to just "noodle around" with a bunch of different notes of your own to make up some of your own patterns. What you've learned so far is enough to begin using this technique in your everyday playing. But there is a lot more that can be done with this technique! So let's get a little fancy....

Everything we've done so far involves leaving the left hand in the same place playing the same two notes. If I were your left hand, I'd be getting pretty bored about now!! Let's try moving the left hand and the right hand to create some moving melodies.

As before, use only the first finger of the right hand. We will first move up and down the D-string to get used to the left hand moving. The purpose of this exercise is to gain control over the left hand as it walks up and down the neck.

After hammering-on a note with the right hand, move the left hand into position for its next note(s). Then do the right-hand pull-off to the left-hand note. The left hand must move quickly, changing position during the time between the right hand's hammer-on and pull-off. Try this....

Exercise 12

Of course, the same kind of ideas apply to the sixteenth-note patterns, as well....

Exercise 13

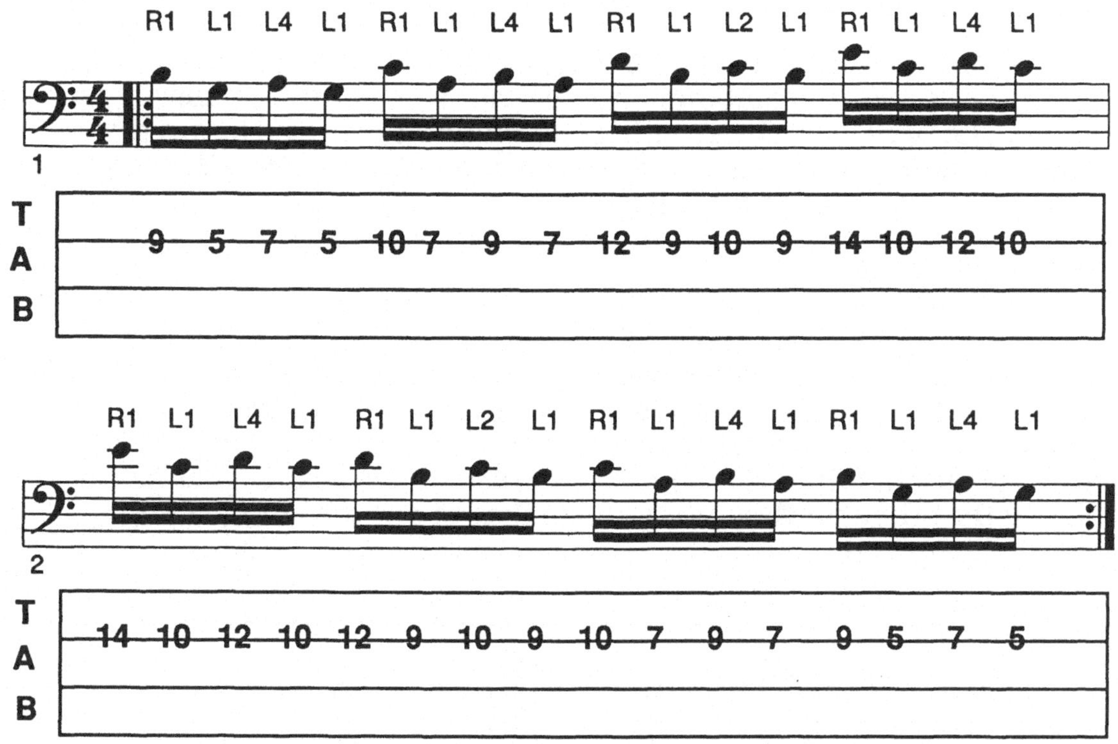

And then there's always....

Exercise 14

Scales and Scale Patterns . . . .

Some of the most creative right-hand hammering lines come from the use of scales in combination with the right-hand hammering technique. The right-hand hammering technique can be used to run through scales at a very quick pace and also to cover larger intervals. Let's take a look at some of the possibilities.

Pentatonic Scales

You remember these, don't you? You did read the previous chapters, didn't you?? When using the right-hand hammering technique to play scales, you are really playing two of the scale positions in one line. Below is a diagram of the E pentatonic scale. The circles represent one scale position, while the squares represent the next higher position. Notice that they overlap. We can use that to our advantage here.

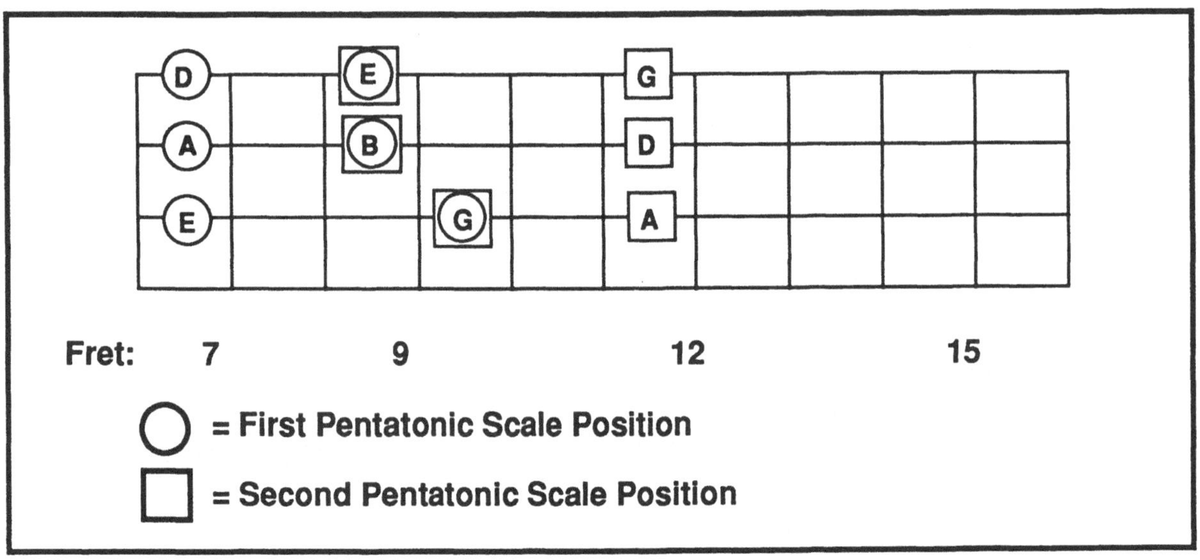

Here are some examples of different ways to play these two scale patterns:

Exercise 14

Exercise 15

Exercise 16

Now let's add the next higher pattern to the picture. Here's a diagram to show you where the scale positions fall:

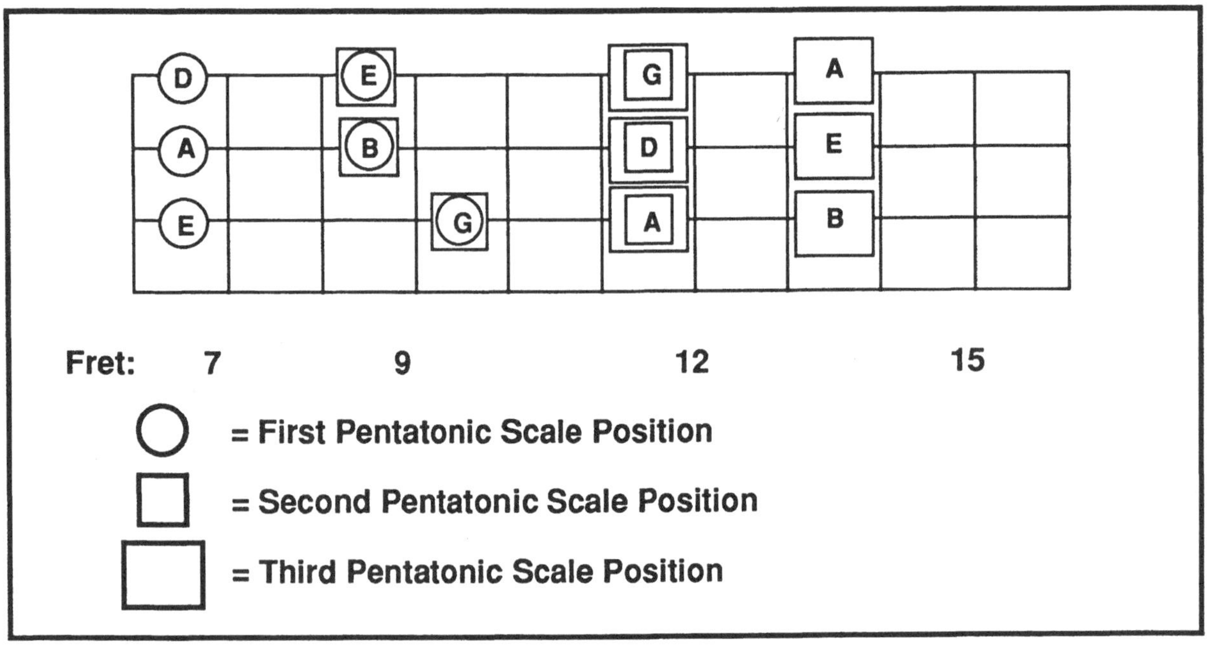

Now we'll play all three patterns together. First, we'll combine all three into one melody line that climbs up through all three. Here are a few examples:

Exercise 17

Exercise 18

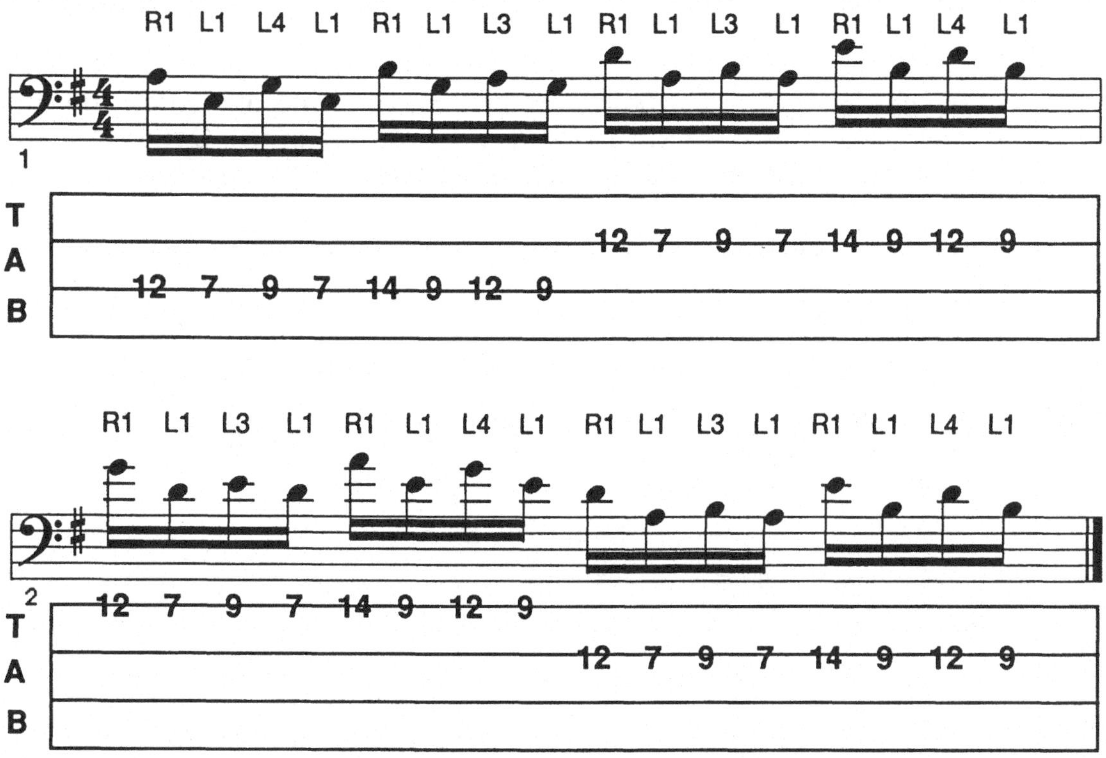

Exercise 19

Getting the idea? You should also experiment with your own melody lines, as there are many, many more than just the few that I'm showing you.

The same type of pattern can be used for major scales, minor scales, harmonic minor, etc.... Below is an example of the C major scale expanded to cover the entire fretboard (or at least one full octave's worth).

Exercise 20

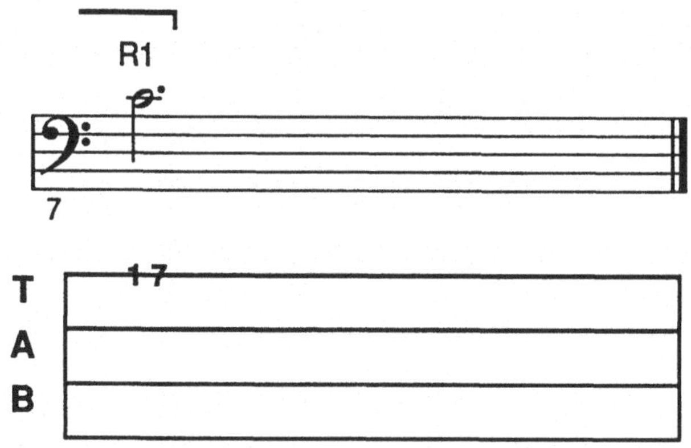

Experiment with some other scale patterns, as well as musical patterns. There are many variations on every pattern you can think of, so play around with some different ideas. I think you'll find that, by doing so, you will be able to create *even more* useful patterns!

Using More Than One Right-Hand Finger ....

Now this whole time that we have been playing these different ideas, you've had three other fingers on your right hand that could have been used to help create wider intervals between notes, help play more notes in a pattern, and even play the patterns more comfortably.

There are actually a couple of ways to play with more than one right-hand finger. One way is to use any one of the four right-hand fingers to play a particular note (i.e. don't always use the first finger on the right hand, but use others, as well). The other way is to play more than one note at a time, using two or more right-hand fingers at once. Let's talk about the first way, using all four fingers to play notes as you please....

As far as the technique goes, each finger on the right hand is used in the same manner. So, in the the following exercises, you should use the same technique for all four fingers as you have been using for the first finger so far.

First we'll look at the technique of using four fingers on the right hand, then we'll get into some examples of melodies and lines that may be played.

The first exercise will help get you used to the idea of using four fingers on the right hand. You will use your left hand to play the notes G, G♯, A, and A♯ on the D-string. The right hand will play the notes B, C, C♯, and D on the D-string, pulling-off to the left-hand notes. Use the first finger on the right hand to play the B; the second finger to play the C; the third to play the C♯; and the fourth to play the D. The exercise is to be played up (B–G–C–G♯–C♯–A–D–A♯) and then back down, without repeating notes. The idea is to get the right-hand fingers to go 1–2–3–4–3–2–1–2–3–4–3–2–1, etc....

Practice this exercise over and over by repeating the phrase until you feel comfortable with it. Here's what it looks like in music and tablature:

Exercise 21

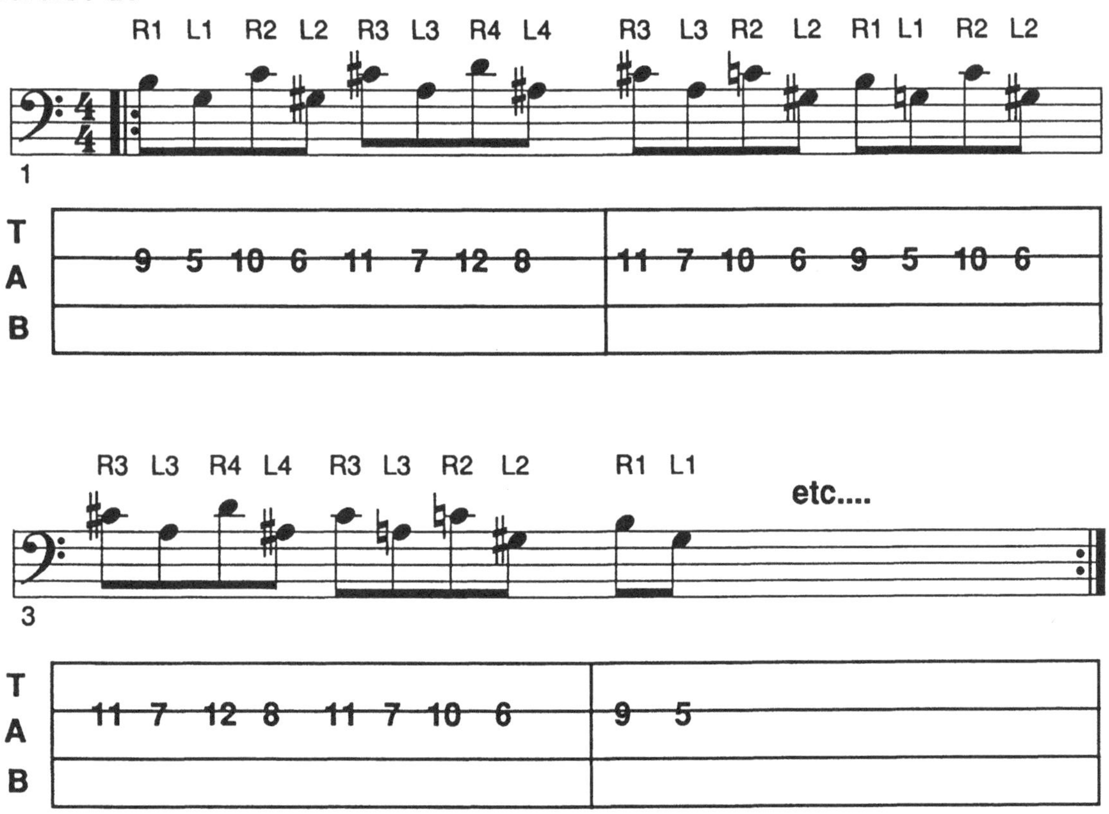

How's that right hand feel? If you're like me, it hurts! The first and second fingers are usually used to picking the strings, so they're pretty strong. But those third and fourth fingers.... Oh, boy!! They are out of shape. Exercises like this are like sending your fingers to an aerobics class! So you should approach these exercises carefully. You want to do them as if you were working out at a gym. Don't try to do too much at first. A little muscle-burn is okay; but, when it gets painful, stop and rest a little. Straining your muscles and tendons will only slow down your progress. Remember, slow down and you'll go faster.

Now let's talk about playing more than one note at a time with the right hand. This technique can be used to create bass lines or solo lines, but it can also be used to "fill out" the bottom by playing double octaves or full chords on the bass.

This first technique involves using two fingers on the right hand to play octaves above two notes (octaves) being played by the left hand. It is really very simple. Let's try it....

Using the first and fourth fingers on your left hand, play the D octave at the 5th fret of the A-string and the 7th fret of the G-string. Now, with the right hand, hammer-on the G at the 10th fret of the A-string with the first finger and the G (octave) at the 12th fret of the G-string with the third finger. Play the D's simultaneously and then play the G's simultaneously. Here's the music and tablature:

Exercise 22

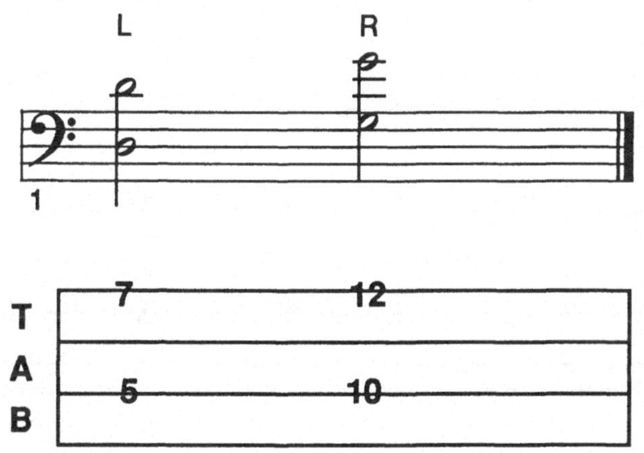

Now try the same thing but, after hammering-on the G octave, pull-off back to the D octave. Like this....

Exercise 23

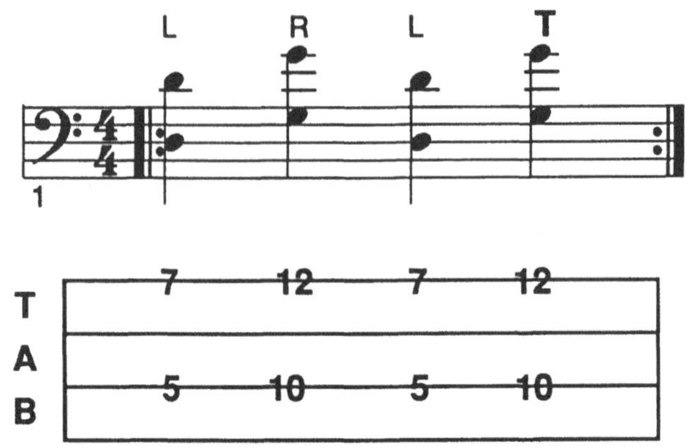

Let's not stop there! Here's an example of a line that could be played using right- and left-hand octaves:

Exercise 24

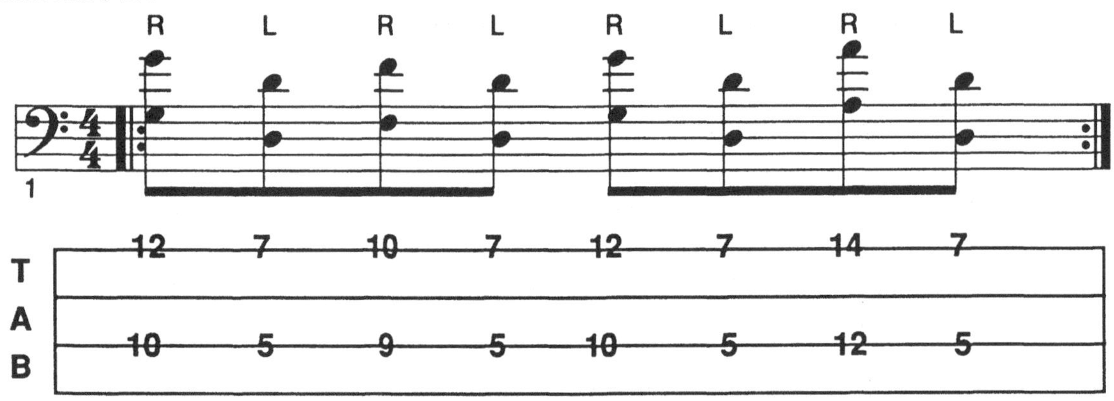

Experiment with different intervals between the right and left hands. That is, in the above exercise, the G octave is a 4th above the D octave; the F is the minor 3rd; the A is the 5th. Try some other intervals to create some different effects.